HOAs Unmasked

What You Can't See Is What Costs You the Most

Bill McKay

Paperback ISBN: 979-8-9959114-1-8

Hardback ISBN: 979-8-9959114-2-5

Published by Doc Vault Inc.

Printed in the United States of America

First Edition

DEDICATION

To the homeowners who pay the bills—thank you.

To the homeowners who have been bullied, targeted, dismissed—labeled, reduced, and made to feel like the problem for simply asking questions. To those who were branded, isolated, and left to navigate what many now understand as HOA syndrome—the quiet weight of confusion, pressure, and powerlessness that too often lives behind closed doors.

This is for you.

To the homeowners who recognize the effort behind the scenes—who thank their board members and property managers, and who choose to engage constructively—you strengthen the system in ways most never see.

To the board members who chose a different path—who took fiduciary duty seriously and carried responsibility not as authority, but as stewardship. And to those across the country who collectively invest millions of volunteer hours each year—often without recognition—working to protect the long-term health of their communities—thank you.

To the property managers in the middle—who absorb pressure from every direction, carry a burden few ever see, and work to improve service and reduce costs in a system that rarely makes it easy—you are seen.

Because the future is already forming—quietly, steadily, inevitably. A future where performance is visible, and accountability is shared, where communities operate as a true system—aligned, informed, and continuously improving.

In that future, doing the right thing is no longer invisible—but expected.

FOREWORD

There were two moments that made the pattern impossible to ignore.

The first was small.

A parking tow sign. The sign had the wrong phone number and the wrong code reference. I had the documentation — clear, specific, directly applicable. I brought it forward expecting a simple correction.

It didn't happen.

The response wasn't that I was wrong. It wasn't that I was right either. It was something in between. The kind of language that acknowledges an issue just enough to move past it — without ever taking a clear position.

The issue didn't get resolved. It didn't escalate either. It stayed in motion.

Emails were acknowledged. Responses were returned. Time passed. Each step gave the appearance of progress without producing a result.

Weeks became months.

At some point, the calculation changes. Not because the issue is no longer real — but because the effort required to keep pushing begins to outweigh the likelihood of anything changing.

That's when most people stop.

Not because they were wrong. Because the system made continuing cost more than letting it go.

At the time, it felt frustrating. In hindsight, it was something else.

The second moment was much larger.

A common area project, roughly $350,000. The recommendation presented to the board stated that vendor references had been checked and job sites had been visited. That was part of the basis for approval.

Later, a few neighbors and I followed up ourselves.

Those visits hadn't happened.

Nothing in the process changed. The contract remained valid. The decision stood. From a procedural standpoint, everything had been done correctly.

But something became clear.

The system had accepted a statement as fact without requiring it to be verified.

There was no mechanism to check it.

The two situations were very different in size. They were identical in structure.

In both cases, I had evidence. In both cases, it didn't change the outcome.

It took time to understand what was actually happening.

I thought the goal was to resolve the issue. The system was operating with a different goal.

The homeowner is trying to fix the problem. The system is trying to contain it.

Both are rational. They're just solving for different outcomes.

That's the disconnect.

Two rational systems. Two different outcomes.

For years, that disconnect has been invisible. Not because anyone intended it to be — but because there has never been a way to measure it.

This book exists because that condition has changed.

CTI™ turns hidden experience into visible signal. The system can no longer ignore it.

What follows is not an argument about bad actors or broken intentions. It is a clear look at a system that has operated without a visible standard — and what becomes possible once that standard exists.

Because once something can be seen, it can be understood.

And once it can be understood, it can be improved.

— **Bill McKay**

Founder, HOA Doctor™

Creator, Community Trust Index™ (CTI™)

Author, HOAs Unmasked

A NOTE ON TERMINOLOGY

Throughout this book, homeowners associations (HOAs), condominium associations (COAs), planned unit developments (PUDs), and community development districts (CDDs) are collectively referred to as the "HOA system," and are analyzed as components of a single structure.

In legal and policy contexts, these structures are more broadly categorized as Common Interest Communities (CICs)—residential frameworks in which property ownership is combined with shared governance, collective financial responsibility, and enforceable community standards.

These structures are not identical. They differ in legal form, governance authority, ownership structure, and how costs are assessed and enforced. In practice, they often operate together—a planned unit development may be governed by an HOA, while a community development district funds and maintains its infrastructure.

For the purposes of this book, these distinctions are acknowledged but not treated as separate systems. They are examined as parts of a single underlying structure: a residential governance system that manages shared property, allocates costs, enforces standards, and shapes the lived experience of homeowners.

The term "HOA system" is used throughout to describe that structure—not to flatten meaningful legal differences, but to focus on the common dynamics that emerge across all of them.

PREFACE

You can learn almost everything about a home before you buy it. Price history, square footage, renovations, school district, and taxes are readily available. The market has made the property visible. What remains out of reach is how the community is actually run. You can inspect the home, but you cannot inspect the system you are buying. That part stays hidden until you are already inside it.

What you are buying is not just a home. It is a system you cannot see.

Once inside, patterns begin to emerge. A maintenance request disappears without resolution, a decision appears finalized before discussion begins, a reserve fund looks adequate until it suddenly isn't, and a special assessment arrives without context. At first, these moments feel isolated—attributable to a bad board, a poor manager, or a one-off issue. Over time, however, the same experiences repeat. They surface in conversations with neighbors, in stories from friends, in other buildings, cities, and states.

The people change. The pattern does not.

The system is active, but it is not being managed at the level it requires. Boards do not fail all at once; they drift. Meetings become procedural, decisions are shaped before they are debated, and input begins to feel like disruption rather than contribution. Confidence evolves into certainty, and certainty gradually resists challenge. At the same time, costs continue to rise—not always because they must, but because no consistent mechanism exists to challenge them. Vendors are approved, budgets are passed, and line items are reviewed, yet performance itself is rarely measured.

The system operates, but it does not improve.

Over time, it becomes less responsive, less efficient, and less accountable to the people funding it.

At its core, an HOA is a business. It manages contracts, vendors, infrastructure, and risk. At the community level, it is responsible for millions of dollars in assets. Across the HOA system, it governs more than $11 trillion in residential value. Yet it is run by volunteers without the structure, standards, or measurement typically required to manage something of that scale. Boards turn over, knowledge does not compound, and each group inherits decisions it did not make and systems it did not design. The institutional memory that could drive improvement never accumulates.

At the same time, management companies operate within a different set of incentives. They are structured to grow portfolios and maintain contracts, while improvement in cost and productivity is rarely measured or required. Performance is reported, but not independently verified, and contracts are renewed without consistent benchmarking. Revenue scales with portfolio size. Improvement does not follow automatically.

The homeowner, who funds the entire system, sits at the edge of it. Concerns move through the same structure being questioned. Requests are processed, issues are acknowledged, but they are rarely converted into measurable change. Over time, homeowners adjust. They engage less—not because the issues disappear, but because the system has not demonstrated that engagement produces results. What appears to be apathy is often something else: a rational response to a system that does not return value for participation.

More than 77 million Americans live in HOA-governed communities. These communities collect over $140 billion in annual dues. Despite this scale, there is no standardized way to measure how they actually perform—not before purchase, not during ownership, and not when critical decisions are being made. What homeowners experience is not random; it is repeatable. Across communities, management companies, and states, the same conditions appear: no defined service standards, no consistent operating procedures, and no structured way to evaluate whether performance improves over time. Boards approve contracts they do not fully understand, deliverables are assumed, and performance remains unmeasured.

I did not set out to write this book. I lived it. As a homeowner within a sub-association, I experienced confusion, misalignment, and a lack of clarity that should not exist in a system managing this level of value. I led a successful board recall seeking change, and afterward returned to being what most participants ultimately are—a homeowner with a clearer understanding of how the system actually functions. At the same time, I served as an officer in a master association overseeing seventeen sub-associations and led a multi-million-dollar community renovation. That experience revealed how these systems operate at scale and how little visibility exists into the outcomes they produce.

What I encountered was not simply poor decisions or bad actors. It was the absence of visibility.

In every system that improves, performance becomes visible. Before that moment, drift appears normal. After that moment, behavior begins to change. HOA communities have never had that moment—until now.

Boards have long defined their communities through mission statements. These statements describe what a community aspires to be—its standards, its values, and its intended character. But they do not measure performance. They express intent; they do not verify outcomes.

The Community Trust Index™ (CTI™) introduces that missing layer. It does not replace vision—it measures it. For the first time, the experience of living in a community can be evaluated, compared, and tracked over time. The standard is no longer what is stated; it is what is demonstrated.

The CTI™ becomes the signal that a community is visible—good, bad, or in between. Participation becomes synonymous with transparency, and transparency becomes expected by the market. Visibility does not destroy value; it reinforces it. Markets do not punish visibility—they price uncertainty. A community that can demonstrate improvement over time becomes more stable, more predictable, and more trusted.

This book is not an attack on HOAs. It is a correction to how they function. Board members, property managers, and homeowners are not adversaries; they are participants in the same system operating without a shared view of performance. When that view exists, alignment follows. Improvement is not optional—it is the standard a board is expected to meet, and it becomes real only when it can be seen, measured, and sustained over time.

The tension that defines so many HOA experiences is not inevitable. It is the result of opacity, and opacity is a solvable problem.

Once the pattern is visible, it cannot be ignored. Once a system can be seen, it begins to change.

And it does not go back.

TABLE OF CONTENTS

PART I – THE PROBLEM

How a system managing $11 trillion in American residential wealth operated for fifty years without a visible standard of accountability

CHAPTER 1

THE SYSTEM YOU CAN'T SEE

The invisible layer shaping property value, daily experience, and long-term financial outcome

The notice arrived in the same stack as everything else—routine, expected, easy to overlook. Nothing about the envelope suggested urgency. It came in the steady rhythm of correspondence that comes with owning a home in a managed community: monthly statements, occasional updates, landscaping schedules. It was opened the same way—casually, without anticipation.

Inside was a single page. At the top, in plain type, was a line that did not match the tone of the envelope it came in.

Special Assessment: $28,000.

She read it once. Then again. Then a third time, more slowly, as if the pace of reading might produce a detail the previous passes had missed—an explanation, a timeline, something that would connect this number to a sequence of decisions that made sense. There was none. The number existed on its own, detached from any visible history, as if it had appeared fully formed rather than accumulated over years through hundreds of small decisions nobody had been watching.

Her first reaction was not panic. It was something more disorienting than panic.

It was confusion.

The building did not feel like it was in distress. The common areas were clean. The landscaping was consistent. Repairs, when needed, had seemed routine. Monthly dues had been paid steadily, every month, for six years, with the assumption that those payments were contributing to a long-term plan—one that accounted for maintenance, repairs, and eventual replacement of shared systems. That assumption had felt so obviously correct that she had never examined it.

Nothing in six years of daily experience had suggested that a financial obligation of this magnitude was building beneath the surface.

And yet it had.

What the notice did not show was the timeline behind it. It did not show the years in which reserve contributions had fallen short—not dramatically, but consistently enough that the gap widened. It did not show the board meetings where the decision was made, again and again, to prioritize dues stability over adequate funding. It did not show the reserve study that had identified the shortfall three years earlier, or the course correction noted in the minutes and never implemented. It did not show the small adjustments—each defensible in the moment—that had gradually created the distance between what was needed and what had been set aside.

That distance had not appeared overnight. It had formed in the space between decisions that each seemed manageable at the time, until the accumulated gap could no longer be absorbed gradually and had to be absorbed all at once.

Now it had a number. And the number had her name on it.

I have seen this number arrive. I have watched what it does to the homeowner who receives it and to the system that produced it. I built this book—and the standard at its center—because the arrival of that number should not be a surprise. It never has needed to be.

THE TRANSACTION THAT STOPPED

In another part of the country, on a different day, a different kind of failure was arriving in a different form.

A home purchase was moving toward completion. The buyer had spent four months searching—navigating listings, attending showings, losing one offer to a competing bid, withdrawing a second after an inspection revealed foundation concerns. The third felt different from the first showing. The unit was right. The neighborhood was right. The price, after negotiation, was right. The inspection came back clean. Financing was secured. Closing felt procedural.

Then the lender paused.

The issue was not the buyer's qualifications. Her credit was strong. Her income was documented. The down payment was in place. The issue was the community the home sat inside.

Late in the process, information surfaced that had existed throughout—embedded in the association's financial records, never fully evaluated. The insurance coverage did not meet the lender's required thresholds. The reserve fund was significantly underfunded—not at the margin, but by a gap the reserve study had been documenting for three years without a corresponding adjustment to contributions. Deferred maintenance had been identified in the most recent inspection report and ignored in the subsequent budget cycle.

None of this was about the property. The unit was in good condition. The building was structurally sound. None of it was about the buyer. She was qualified, prepared, and ready to close.

What changed was that the information finally arrived. And when it did, it arrived too late.

The lender reassessed its exposure and declined to proceed. From the outside, it looked like a buyer who had done everything right, losing a home she had earned. What it actually was: a late discovery. The records that would have changed the outcome had been sitting in a filing cabinet the entire time—organized into nothing a buyer could act on before the offer, before the inspection, before sixty days of financial and emotional investment.

She did not get the home.

THE NOTICE THAT ARRIVED WITHOUT CONTEXT

A third homeowner, in a third community, experienced a smaller version of the same structural pattern. Not a $28,000 assessment. Not a collapsed transaction. Something quieter—and in some ways more representative of how the system operates for most people inside it.

A violation notice arrived for something that had been consistent and unchanged for years. The item in question—a planter on the balcony, a doormat outside the unit, a storage arrangement identical since the day he moved in—had generated no concern in three years of ownership. No conversation, no warning, no indication that anything was out of compliance.

Then the notice arrived.

He called the management company to understand what had changed. The call was not returned. He sent an email. An automated acknowledgment arrived. He followed up. Three weeks later, a second notice arrived. This one included a fine.

What stood out was not the amount. It was the sequence. He had tried to engage before the consequence arrived—reached out before the fine, looking for the conversation that would let him resolve the issue. The system was not available for that conversation. It appeared only when it was ready to act, not when he was ready to engage.

A governance system organized around its own operational convenience rather than around the homeowner it is meant to serve produces exactly this experience—every day, in communities across the country.

FOUR STORIES, ONE STRUCTURE

Taken individually, these situations appear unrelated. They differ in scale, in financial impact, in the personalities involved and the communities they occurred in. What connects them is not the outcome. It is the structure behind the outcome.

In each case, the system was active. Decisions were being made. Money was moving. What was missing was a clear and accessible connection between what the system was doing and what that meant for the person funding it.

The homeowner who received the assessment had been paying into a system whose financial trajectory she could not see. The buyer who lost the transaction had been evaluating a community whose governance condition she could not access. The homeowner who received the violation notice had been living inside a system whose enforcement priorities were invisible until they were applied.

A fourth buyer—in a fourth community—experienced a failure that did not involve governance at all. Or so it appeared.

The closing was scheduled for Friday morning. Furniture had been measured. Utilities arranged. The lender had issued final approval. The title company had circulated the closing disclosure. At that point in a transaction, nothing is supposed to go wrong.

Then the title company called.

The warranty deed contained an inconsistency carried forward from a prior transaction—a description that did not fully match the recorded boundaries, a prior correction noted but never properly recorded. A chain of documents that, read in sequence, left just enough ambiguity that the title insurer could not certify ownership without qualification.

It was not fraud. It was not even unusual. It was a small error, introduced at some point in the property's history, never resolved because nothing had required it to be.

Until now.

The closing did not happen on Friday. She had done everything right. The condition had been present the entire time—carried forward from one transaction to the next because nothing in the system required it to surface until the moment when surfacing it stopped everything.

Four different outcomes. The same underlying absence.

These situations feel isolated when they occur. The assessment feels like a financial failure specific to this board, this period of governance. The failed transaction feels like bad timing, a particular lender's particular threshold. The violation notice feels personal.

They are not isolated. They emerge from the same underlying structure—one that operates across communities regardless of size, location, or management approach. A structure that has been accumulating consequence for fifty years without a standard by which that consequence could be measured, predicted, or addressed before it arrived.

THE SCALE OF THE INVISIBLE

More than 77 million Americans live in communities governed by homeowners associations. Not a niche market. Not a demographic segment. The largest single housing category in the United States, spanning every price range, every building type, every region of the country.

These communities represent more than $11 trillion in residential property value. Each year, homeowners contribute more than $140 billion in dues to support maintenance, operations, reserves, insurance, and shared infrastructure. That figure exceeds the GDP of most countries. It is one of the largest ongoing transfers of residential wealth in the American economy—flowing through a system that has never had a standardized, externally verified performance standard against which its use could be measured.

More than 67 percent of newly constructed homes in the United States are built inside HOA communities. The percentage has been rising for decades. The homeowners entering this system for the first time every year are entering without the information infrastructure that every other major market has developed—without a signal that tells them, before they commit, what they are actually buying into.

HOA governance is how decisions are made, how money is managed, and how rules are created and enforced over time. Those decisions shape not only daily operations but the long-term risk, cost, and value of the property itself. A board that funds reserves adequately protects homeowners from future assessments. A board that consistently defers maintenance is not reducing cost—it is converting it into a larger, more urgent expense that will arrive later. A management company that responds to maintenance requests preserves value through daily execution. One that absorbs requests without acting erodes that value, quietly, one unresolved issue at a time.

These decisions compound. At the scale of an estimated 40 million homes and $140 billion in annual dues, small differences in governance quality do not remain small for long. A community paying above-market rates for vendor contracts—in the absence of competitive benchmarking—is losing real money every year across every homeowner who funds it.

Across the system, that inefficiency is not a rounding error. At the higher end of informed estimates, the annual cost of governance without accountability approaches $28 billion—driven by overrun projects, redo work, above-market vendor pricing, deferred maintenance, and avoidable legal and operational costs.

Twenty-eight billion dollars. Not lost in dramatic fraud or obvious negligence. Lost in the ordinary accumulation of small decisions made without consequence—in the space the absence of a performance standard creates and sustains.

THE ARCHITECTURE OF THE INVISIBLE

The natural question is why. How does a system managing this much money, affecting this many people, operate for fifty years without a standard?

The answer is not corruption. The answer is structure—and what happened to it as scale arrived.

The HOA system was built to serve homeowners. In its original form—small communities, volunteer boards, direct accountability between decision-maker and consequence—it did. The board member who approved the maintenance deferral lived with the result. The neighbor who accepted a governance role understood that the decision made at Tuesday's meeting would affect the building she walked into Wednesday morning. Accountability was not formal. It was proximity. And proximity, when it exists, does not require a standard to keep a system honest.

What happened over fifty years is that the system scaled without its accountability mechanisms scaling with it. Communities grew from eighty units to eight hundred to eight thousand. Professional management replaced volunteer administration. The board member who once lived inside every consequence now governs a community large enough that the gap between decision and outcome is measured in years. The management company that once operated in a single building now manages a portfolio of forty-three.

Each change was rational. Each was driven by scale, and scale was driven by demand. To deliver amenities, maintenance, and shared infrastructure at scale required the professionalization that produced the distance. The distance is not a design flaw. It is a design consequence.

But consequence has its own consequences.

The board approving the maintenance contract is approving the recommendation of the management company that selected the vendor. The homeowner paying monthly dues is funding a process whose results remain invisible until they arrive as a special assessment, a failed closing, or a violation notice without context. The system reorganized itself—gradually, without announcement—around operational efficiency. Not as a policy. As a progression. And once it had reorganized, the feedback loops that proximity once created for free were gone. Nothing was built to replace them.

The result is a system in which performance varies enormously—across communities, across management companies, across time within the same community—with no shared reference point against which that variation can be seen, measured, or corrected.

WHY SPECIAL ASSESSMENTS FEEL SUDDEN WHEN THEY AREN'T

Boards make decisions under two competing pressures. The first is the obligation to fund future needs adequately—to set reserve contributions at levels that match the projected cost of replacing shared components over time. The second is the immediate, visible pressure to keep current dues stable. Homeowners want low dues. They vote for board members who deliver them. They attend annual meetings and ask why the budget is increasing. They do not, in general, ask whether the reserve fund is on a trajectory to meet projected costs in ten years.

Between those two pressures, boards choose. Across the country, the choice that preserves relationships and produces the smoothest annual meeting is the choice that prioritizes dues stability. The contribution rate holds steady. The reserve fund grows more slowly than projected needs. The gap widens—not dramatically in any single year, but consistently—until it is no longer a planning problem and has become a financial reality.

That financial reality arrives as a special assessment. And it feels sudden because, for the homeowner who was never shown the trajectory, it was.

The cost had been building for years in a document no one was required to explain and few thought to request. The reserve study that told the story was technically available. The financial statements that showed the trajectory were technically disclosed. What was never built was the mechanism to turn that information into something a homeowner could use at the moment using it would have mattered.

That is the structural condition this book addresses. Not concealment. The absence of a translation layer between what the system knows and what the homeowner can act on—and the $28 billion in annual waste that accumulates in that absence, across 77 million homes, through the ordinary operation of a system that was never required to close the gap.

THE PATTERN THAT REPEATS

The Surfside condominium collapse in June 2021 was an extreme outcome. Ninety-eight people died in the sudden failure of a building that had been standing for forty years. The investigation worked backward from the failure—not to find the moment the building came down, but to trace the sequence that preceded it. What investigators found was not a sudden catastrophic event concealed within a stable system. It was a condition that had been present, documented, and understood in fragments—for years—without ever being organized into a picture that required decisive action.

Water intrusion had been observed. Cracking had developed in load-bearing connections. Protective systems had weakened. Recommendations had been made. Some were acted on. Others were deferred because the condition had not yet reached the threshold the system recognized as requiring immediate response. Decisions were made in good faith, within a structure not designed to produce the comprehensive view that might have changed them.

The visible outcome was sudden. The sequence that produced it was not.

Surfside is the most dramatic expression of a pattern that plays out in communities across the country every year, at different scales and with less catastrophic consequences. A condition is identified. The comprehensive solution carries a cost the current board is reluctant to recommend. The incremental response is chosen. The condition continues to develop. The cost compounds until the solution is no longer optional—it is urgent, expensive, and arrives as a concentrated burden on homeowners who funded the deferred decisions.

The homeowner who receives the assessment did not choose the deferral. She may not have known about it. She was living inside the system that made the choice and inheriting its consequence—the way all HOA homeowners inherit governance decisions made before them, around them, and without their knowledge.

HOW RESPONSIBILITY IS DISTRIBUTED

What makes this pattern difficult to address is not the absence of people responsible for preventing it. It is the distribution of responsibility across roles that see different parts of the system and are accountable to different things.

The board is responsible for governance—setting direction and approving decisions that shape the community's long-term condition. Board members are volunteers. They serve because they care, because no one else stepped forward, or because a neighbor asked. They are not, in most cases, engineers or financial analysts. They evaluate recommendations made by the management company using information the management company has organized.

The management company is responsible for execution—implementing the board's decisions and coordinating day-to-day operations. Management companies bring professional systems and expertise that volunteer boards cannot replicate. They also manage portfolios—forty communities, sixty, a hundred—that make deep knowledge of any individual community increasingly difficult to maintain as scale grows.

Vendors provide the services that support the community's physical condition, selected through processes the management company organizes and evaluated against standards the management company defines.

Each role is necessary. Each operates within a defined frame. And each, operating within that frame, can produce a picture of community performance that looks reasonable from the inside—while the homeowner's experience of the same system looks entirely different.

The board can point to the decisions it approved. The management company can point to the processes it executed. The vendor can point to the work it performed. And the homeowner, at the end of those correct and defensible explanations, is sitting with a number that none of them adequately accounts for.

That is the governance gap. Not a failure of any individual. A failure of the system to connect its parts in a way that produces accountability where it matters most—to the homeowner.

THE GAP THAT HAS A COST

This gap is not a philosophical problem. It arrives in mailboxes and at closing tables. It arrives as maintenance requests that disappear, violation notices that appear without warning, and financial reports that satisfy a disclosure requirement without informing the person who reads them.

The homeowner who cannot see the reserve trajectory cannot ask about it before the assessment arrives. The buyer who cannot assess governance quality cannot price the risk before making an offer. The board member with no external reference point cannot know whether the community she governs is performing above or below what comparable communities are actually achieving. The management company whose performance is measured only by instruments it produced cannot see the distance between what it believes it is delivering and what verified homeowners describe as their experience.

Each of these is a real cost. Some arrive as dollars. Some arrive as decisions made without information that would have changed them. Some arrive as the gradual erosion of community trust—the homeowner who disengages after one too many unanswered requests, replaced by the silence that allows governance to drift further from accountability.

Fifty years of performance, varying enormously across communities and over time within communities, without a standard against which that variation could be measured or corrected.

What has been missing is not the information. The information has always existed—in reserve studies, financial statements, maintenance logs, and vendor contracts. What has been missing is the mechanism that turns information into signal: a consistent, comparable, externally visible measure of how a community is actually performing.

That mechanism is now being built. The chapters that follow trace how, and why it changes everything.

The notice arrived in the same stack as everything else. Routine. Expected. Easy to overlook.

It should not have been a surprise. The information that would have made it predictable had existed for years—in documents the system produced, organized into forms the system understood, and held in a structure the homeowner had no reliable way to read.

What was missing was never the information. It was the standard that would have organized it into something she could use—before the envelope arrived, before the number appeared, before the consequence became hers to absorb.

That standard now exists.

CHAPTER 2

THE ORIGINAL IDEA

What the homeowners association was designed to do–and the community it was built to protect

The gap Chapter One describes did not arrive with the modern HOA. It arrived when the modern HOA diverged from the original one. Understanding how that divergence happened—and what it cost—requires going back to what the model was actually designed to do.

The street was finished on a Tuesday in the spring of 1964.

He had watched it go in—the paving crew, the curb forms, the sod laid in long rolls along the easement separating road from homes. His was the fourteenth of thirty-two in a new development outside Phoenix, built by a developer who had noticed that veterans coming back from Korea and their younger brothers finishing college were looking for something old neighborhoods did not offer. Space. Newness. A community that felt designed rather than accumulated.

The development had a pool. It had a small park where the streets converged near the entrance. It had landscaping along the common areas that the developer's brochure described as professionally maintained—and that he understood, when he signed, to mean it would stay the way it looked in the brochure.

What made it stay that way was the association.

Not a government. Not a landlord. Neighbors governing what they shared. Pooling a modest monthly contribution to pay for maintenance, electing three of their own to oversee how it was spent, and trusting the mechanism because the mechanism was themselves—thirty-two households who had all made the same bet on the same street and had every reason to want it to hold its value.

The first board meeting was held in his living room. Twelve people attended. They argued about the landscaping budget for forty minutes and agreed on a number nobody was fully satisfied with and everybody could live with. Then they went home.

It was not sophisticated. It did not need to be. It worked because everyone in the room would be walking past the landscaping the next morning.

THE PROMISE

The homeowners association did not begin as a governance system. It began as a promise.

When the first large-scale planned communities were built in postwar America, the association was conceived as the mechanism that would allow neighbors to steward what they shared—the roads, the parks, the common spaces that gave the development its character and its value. Owners would contribute to a common fund, elect representatives from among themselves, and those representatives would make decisions about the shared environment in the interest of everyone who lived inside it.

The promise had three parts. Maintenance: the shared physical environment would be kept in the condition that had attracted buyers to it in the first place. Fairness: the rules governing the community would apply equally to everyone, without favoritism or exception. Stewardship: the money contributed by homeowners would be managed carefully, with the long-term health of the community as the governing priority.

These three promises were not written into the governing documents with that simplicity. They were embedded in the structure of the original model in a way that made them feel less like promises and more like inevitabilities. The board member who approved the maintenance contract was the same person who walked past the results every morning. The homeowner who raised a concern at the board meeting was raising it in a room where everyone knew everyone. The money being managed was the money of neighbors, spent on things neighbors could see, accountable to people who would encounter each other at the mailbox.

The governance was not formal. It was proximity. And proximity, at the right scale, does the work of a thousand governance frameworks without requiring any of them.

WHAT PROXIMITY ACTUALLY PROVIDED

Proximity provided three things the modern system has struggled to replace: information, feedback, and consequence.

The board member who lived in the community had direct, daily access to what governance required. She did not need a report to know whether the landscaping contract was being fulfilled. She walked past the landscaping. She did not need a management company summary to know whether the pool was being maintained. She used the pool. The gap between what the system was doing and what the people governing it knew about it was essentially zero.

When a governance decision produced a bad outcome, she heard about it—not through a formal complaint process, but through the parking lot conversation, the mailbox encounter, the neighborly exchange that is impossible to avoid in a community of thirty-two homes. The feedback loop was short, personal, and unavoidable.

And when she made a poor financial decision, she did not receive a negative performance review. She lived with the outcome. Her property value was tied to the same long-term trajectory as every other owner in the community. The consequence of poor governance was personal, immediate, and impossible to outsource.

When the same person makes the decision and lives with the result, governance tends to be honest. Not perfect. Honest.

These three elements—information, feedback, and consequence—are what proximity created for free. They are also what the system lost as it scaled. And they are precisely what the verified homeowner signal is built to restore.

THE ORIGINAL CONTRACT

The original HOA operated as something closer to a compact than a governance structure. Homeowners joined not because they were required to—in the early years, many associations were voluntary—but because the shared investment in the common environment was visible and the benefit of maintaining it was obvious. The dues were modest. The decisions were local. The accountability was immediate and personal.

Board members were accountable because they were neighbors. Not in a theoretical, institutional sense. In a daily, face-to-face, I-see-you-at-the-mailbox sense that no governance document has ever replicated. When something went wrong, everyone knew. When something went right, the people responsible for it heard about it.

The community that operated this way produced something easy to undervalue until it disappears: a shared environment that people felt genuine ownership over. Not legal ownership—most homeowners understood the distinction between their unit and the common areas they collectively maintained. Felt ownership. The kind that produces voluntary participation, community investment, and the neighbor who shovels the sidewalk in front of the building even when their own unit is thirty feet away.

That felt ownership was not incidental to the association's success. It was the source of it. Communities where residents felt genuinely connected to the shared environment maintained it better, funded it more adequately, participated more consistently, and produced the long-term property value stability that had attracted buyers to them in the first place.

Take away the felt ownership and you do not merely lose participation. You lose the maintenance. You lose the funding. You lose the long-term stability. What remains is a governance structure that looks identical to the one that worked and produces outcomes that look nothing like it.

That is precisely what happened as the system scaled.

WHAT MADE THE ORIGINAL MODEL WORK

Three structural conditions created the environment in which the original HOA fulfilled its promise. They were not designed in as conscious features. They were what the scale of the early association made natural.

The first was scale. Early associations were small enough that every board member had direct, personal knowledge of what the community needed. Decisions did not travel through layers of reporting before reaching the people responsible for making them.

The second was transparency—not in the modern, document-disclosure sense, but in the organic sense that comes from living inside a small community where information moves through conversation and observation. Homeowners knew what was being spent because they could see what was being built. They knew what was being deferred because they could see what was being ignored.

The third was consequence. The board member who made a poor financial decision lived with the outcome. Her property value was tied to the same long-term trajectory as every other owner. The consequence of poor governance was personal, immediate, and impossible to outsource.

Scale, transparency, and consequence. These three conditions created the feedback loops that kept the original HOA honest. Remove any one of them and the system begins to drift. Remove all three—as the modern large-scale managed community effectively has—and the system that remains looks structurally identical to the original while producing outcomes the original could not have sustained.

THE SEED OF EVERYTHING THAT FOLLOWED

The original design also contained the seed of everything that followed. Not a flaw, exactly. A tension. A structural feature that made the model replicable at scale while making the conditions that made it work increasingly difficult to preserve as it grew.

The HOA was built to replicate. The model that worked for eighty homes in a 1960s subdivision was intended to work for eight hundred homes in a 1990s master-planned community, and then for eight thousand homes in a 2010s mega-development. The documents replicated. The structures replicated. The legal frameworks were standardized across states. Developer after developer adopted the model because it solved a real problem—how to maintain shared infrastructure in a community of private owners—at a price point buyers could absorb and a governance structure regulators could recognize.

What did not replicate was proximity.

You cannot legislate proximity. You cannot standardize it or include it as a clause in the CC&Rs. Proximity is what happens when the person making the decision and the person living with its consequence are the same person—or close enough that the distance between them creates natural accountability without requiring formal structures to maintain it.

As communities grew, the three conditions proximity had sustained began to erode. Scale increased beyond the point where board members could have direct knowledge of every homeowner's experience. Transparency gave way to formal reporting. Consequence became attenuated as the distance between decision-maker and outcome grew—as terms ended, boards rotated, and the person who had approved the deferred maintenance was no longer serving when it produced its cost.

The model continued to spread. The accountability that had made it work continued to thin. And the gap between what the model promised and what it was producing continued to widen, quietly, in the space that the absence of proximity created and the absence of a standard allowed to persist.

THE TRANSITION NOBODY ANNOUNCED

There was no single moment when the HOA system stopped being organized around homeowner experience and started being organized around operational efficiency. No announcement. No policy change. No regulatory shift that redefined the relationship between the person who governed and the person who paid.

The transition happened through accumulation. Each new community was slightly larger than the ones that came before. Each successive wave of development brought professional management into communities previously governed by volunteers. Each contract that replaced a volunteer function with a professional service added a layer of structure between the homeowner and the decision that shaped their daily experience.

The management company that took over administration from the volunteer committee brought expertise and process. It also brought distance. The manager handling twelve communities could not know any of them the way the volunteer who lived in one had known it. The standardized maintenance ticketing system that replaced the informal work order was more consistent and less human. The financial reporting that satisfied regulatory requirements communicated less to the homeowner who received it than the annual meeting conversation had communicated to their predecessor.

Each of these changes was defensible. Most were genuine improvements along some dimension. The dimension along which none of them were improvements was the feedback loop.

The volunteer board member who lived in the community had an unavoidable feedback loop built into her daily existence. The professional management company had no such loop. Its feedback came through formal channels—service calls, complaint submissions, contract reviews—organized around the management company's operational convenience rather than around the homeowner's lived experience.

By the time the transition was complete, most of the people operating inside the system had never known anything else. The boards governing large communities had never experienced the direct feedback that kept early associations accountable. The management companies executing governance decisions had never operated in an environment where their performance was immediately visible to the people who paid for it.

The model had scaled. The accountability had not.

WHAT THE ORIGINAL IDEA STILL GETS RIGHT

The original idea was not wrong. It was incomplete.

The concept of shared governance—neighbors pooling resources to maintain what they share, electing representatives to manage that process, holding those representatives accountable through the mechanisms of community ownership—is sound. Where it has been preserved with genuine fidelity to its original intent, it produces communities that are well-maintained, financially stable, and deeply satisfying to live in.

The evidence is visible in every well-run HOA in the country. Communities where boards take the fiduciary duty seriously, where management companies compete on service quality rather than relationship depth, where homeowners participate because participation produces results. These communities exist in every market, at every price point, in every building type.

What the original design lacked was the ability to preserve accountability at scale. It depended on proximity to create the feedback loops that proximity no longer reliably creates once a community grows beyond the size where daily interaction between decision-maker and outcome is natural. It had no mechanism to replace what proximity provided when proximity disappeared.

The governing documents were replicated. The governance structure was replicated. The dues mechanism was replicated. What was not replicated was the proximity that had made the original model honest.

Those documents were written at a point in time—often decades earlier—before many of the conditions communities now face even existed. Short-term rentals, platform-driven occupancy, modern insurance volatility, and the scale of today's vendor ecosystems were not part of the environment those documents were designed to govern. The framework remained fixed. The system it governed did not.

Proximity cannot be replicated through documents. It can only be replicated through a mechanism that performs the same function—one that creates the information, feedback, and consequence that proximity once created naturally.

That mechanism is what the CTI™ is built to provide. Not a replacement for community governance. A replacement for the proximity that made community governance work—and that the scale of the modern HOA system has made impossible to recreate naturally.

The original idea was right. The infrastructure to sustain it at scale simply did not exist yet.

It does now.

He is in his eighties now, if he is still alive. The development outside Phoenix where he watched the street go in was sold and absorbed into a larger master-planned community sometime in the late 1980s. The original thirty-two homes are still there, according to the records, surrounded by three hundred more built in the decade after.

The board meeting in his living room was not the last one. For twenty years, the association he helped found governed the development the way it had been designed to be governed—personally, locally, with the kind of accountability that comes from knowing the people you are deciding for will see you tomorrow.

That accountability was not a policy. It was a condition. And the condition, once gone—replaced by a professional management structure that served the expanded community efficiently and knew it less intimately—could not be recovered by wanting it back.

What could be recovered was the function it served. The feedback it created. The consequence it made unavoidable. Not through proximity. Through a verified signal that performs the same work at a scale proximity never could.

The promise the original HOA made—maintenance, fairness, stewardship—has not changed. What has changed is the availability of the mechanism that makes the promise verifiable.

CHAPTER 3

THE SHIFT NO ONE NOTICED

How the system that worked at thirty-two homes stopped working at three thousand

The light fixture had been out for eleven days.

It was not an emergency. It was a hallway fixture on the second floor of a mid-rise condominium — dim enough to notice every time he walked past it, not dark enough to be dangerous. The kind of thing that gets fixed in a well-run building within a week and in a poorly run one within a month and in most buildings somewhere in between, depending on factors the homeowner cannot see and was rarely designed to see.

He called the number listed in the management company's correspondence. A recorded greeting informed him that his call was important, guided him through a menu, and connected him to a voicemail. He left a message with his unit number, contact information, and a description of the problem. He ended the call believing the request had entered the system.

Three days later, the light was still out. No acknowledgment, no callback, no confirmation that the message had reached anyone. He called again, reached a person, who transferred him to another person, who told him the request had been logged and would be assigned to a technician. He asked when. The person said they could not give a timeline, but someone would follow up.

No one followed up.

He was not angry yet. He was paying attention. He noticed, for the first time with real precision, the architecture of the system he was trying to reach — the number of steps between his call and a human being, the number of people between that human being and the one who would actually fix the light, the distance between the moment he identified a problem and the moment anyone in the system would experience a consequence for it remaining unresolved.

That distance was the thing he had not previously thought to measure.

He had lived in the building for four years. He had paid dues every month. He had attended two annual meetings and found them informative in the way that reading minutes of a meeting you were not fully present for is informative — technically accurate, contextually thin. He had assumed, without ever examining the assumption, that the system managing his building was organized around his needs. That when something went wrong, the path from problem to resolution was clear, short, and accountable to someone who would feel the consequence of it remaining unresolved.

What he was discovering, eleven days into a burned-out hallway light, was that the path was none of those things.

He fixed it himself. He bought a bulb, found the maintenance closet unlocked on a Thursday afternoon, and changed it. Eight minutes.

But the question he was left with did not have a hardware store solution.

When did the system stop being organized around me?

BEHIND THE CURTAIN

At first glance, most homeowners assume their community is managed locally. A board of neighbors makes decisions. A management company handles operations. Vendors perform services as needed. It feels contained. Accountability feels roughly direct.

Beneath that surface, the structure is far more layered than most homeowners — and many board members — understand. Across the country, a significant portion of HOA, COA, and CDD communities are supported by large regional and national management organizations that operate across hundreds or thousands of associations. These firms provide essential services: financial management, vendor coordination, compliance support, operational continuity. They have built platforms, systems, and processes that no volunteer board could replicate.

Over the past two decades, the industry has consolidated significantly. Smaller, independent firms built on local relationships and community-specific knowledge have been acquired by or integrated into larger platforms. The relationships between boards, management companies, and vendors have become more interconnected, more standardized, and — from the homeowner's perspective — less transparent.

This evolution brought consistency, resources, and professionalization to communities that had previously relied entirely on volunteer capacity. It also introduced structure. And structure, in any system involving money, services, and multiple parties with different interests, shapes outcomes in ways that are not always legible from the outside.

The result is not a single problem. It is a system where accountability is diffuse and performance is difficult to assess from the outside. This is the curtain — not something hidden by design, but something that has rarely been fully illuminated.

WHAT PROXIMITY DID

The board member in Phoenix governed thirty-two homes from his living room. He did not need a ticketing system. He did not need a performance report. When the landscaping looked bad, he knew. When a neighbor was unhappy, he heard. When a decision had produced the wrong outcome, he felt it — because he lived inside it.

That is what made the system honest. Not the governing documents. Not the fiduciary duty framework. The unavoidable fact that the person making the decision was the same person living with the result.

When proximity disappeared — when communities grew large enough that board members no longer had direct, daily contact with the outcomes of their decisions, and when professional management replaced the volunteer function that had kept decision-makers physically inside the system they governed — something entered the space proximity had occupied.

But what entered was not the same thing.

WHAT ENTERED THE SPACE

When proximity disappeared, professional management filled the gap. Not imposed from outside — required by scale. Communities grew beyond the size where volunteer administration was practical. Decisions became too numerous, too technical, and too consequential to be handled part-time by neighbors with day jobs. The management company filled a real gap.

But filling a gap and replacing what was lost are not the same thing.

The volunteer board member had one incentive: live well in the community she governed. Her interest and the community's interest were structurally identical. The roof she maintained adequately was the roof over her own unit. The reserve fund she managed responsibly was the fund that would protect her own investment.

The management company has a different incentive. It is a business. Its primary obligation is to its own financial health, which depends on maintaining contracts, managing operations efficiently across a portfolio, and keeping the boards that renew those contracts satisfied. These are legitimate business objectives. They are not the same as the homeowner's objective, which is to live in a well-governed community whose shared assets are maintained and whose financial management is sound.

Both incentives are rational. They are not aligned. And misaligned incentives, operating inside a system where the party with more expertise sets the terms of the relationship, tend to produce outcomes that serve the better-positioned party — not through malice, but through the ordinary operation of a system organized around execution rather than accountability.

The management company managing forty-three communities is organized around managing forty-three communities efficiently. Not around the daily experience of the homeowner in Unit 412 who submitted a maintenance request three weeks ago and has not heard back. Both can be true simultaneously. The company can be operating exactly as designed and the homeowner can be experiencing exactly the gap that the design produces.

That gap is what happened to the feedback loop.

THE SHIFT

The shift was not the arrival of professional management. Done well, professional management serves communities better than volunteer administration at scale. The shift was the change in feedback.

In the early model, feedback was immediate. The board member who made a decision that affected her neighbors heard about it, because her neighbors were the people she lived among. The feedback was personal. It was unavoidable.

In the professional management model, feedback became delayed. It arrived through service calls logged into ticketing systems, through complaints submitted via email to addresses that routed to centralized service centers, through annual meeting comments that were received and noted and addressed or not depending on whether addressing them was operationally convenient. Feedback that had once been personal became contractual.

The homeowner who had once experienced immediate, personal accountability from her board was now experiencing delayed, institutional responsiveness from a management company. The experience was different in kind, not just in degree — not slower service from the same kind of system, but a different kind of system entirely. One that processed requests rather than responded to neighbors. That managed relationships rather than maintained communities. That was accountable to contract terms rather than to the daily experience of the people whose dues funded everything.

I have sat in that board meeting where the decision was framed before the discussion began. The agenda item that appeared to offer three options had two options and a recommendation. The recommendation had already incorporated the constraints that would make the other two difficult to choose. The board voted. The outcome was already shaped. What looked like governance was the execution of a decision made one layer below.

Nobody in the room was acting in bad faith. The management company had done the work of preparing the options. The board was doing the work of reviewing and approving them. Both were operating exactly as designed. The design just no longer produced the feedback loop that proximity had once created for free.

THE DISTANCE THAT FOLLOWED

Each layer of professional management added distance between the homeowner's experience and the system's response. Each layer made operational sense. Together, they changed the system in ways nobody designed and nobody announced.

Managers began handling more communities. Their knowledge of any single community became broader and less deep. The manager who had once known a building the way a resident knows it — its recurring issues, its difficult personalities, its seasonal maintenance patterns, the elevator that always acts up in August — was replaced by a manager who knew the ticketing system for forty communities and knew none of them the way someone who lived there would know it.

Response times that had once been measured in hours extended to days, then weeks. Communication that had once been personal became standardized — templates replacing conversations, automated acknowledgments replacing actual contact, form letters replacing the exchange between a person with a problem and a person with the ability to resolve it.

The homeowner felt it before she could define it. The building felt different. Not dramatically worse — not in any way that would produce a formal complaint. Just more distant. More transactional. More like an institution processing a request than a community responding to a neighbor.

That last part — impossible to measure — is the condition that allowed the drift to continue. In every other domain where service quality matters, the gap between what a provider believes it is delivering and what its customers are actually experiencing eventually produces a corrective signal: a declining rating, a lost contract, a pattern of complaints that requires a response. In the HOA system, that signal did not exist. The homeowner's experience was private. It lived in her apartment and her conversations with neighbors and her diminishing willingness to submit maintenance requests that seemed unlikely to be addressed.

The homeowner experiences the outcome. The system experiences the report. The gap between those two becomes the defining feature of how the system operates.

THE ACCOUNTABILITY THAT PROXIMITY PROVIDED FOR FREE

There is a precise way to describe what was lost when proximity disappeared: the feedback loop that kept governance quality from drifting in the direction of whatever was most convenient for the parties responsible for producing it.

In the early model, that feedback loop existed because the board member who made a governance decision lived inside its consequence. She had no ability to avoid the information her decision had produced. The feedback was automatic, immediate, and personal.

In the modern model, that feedback loop must be created artificially — through formal mechanisms, external standards, verified signals that perform the function proximity once performed. The board that does not create those mechanisms governs without feedback. The management company not required to produce its performance against a verified external standard operates without the signal that would require it to adjust. The vendor whose work is never measured against anything except the management company's own report delivers whatever it delivers, at whatever cost, into a system with no mechanism for knowing whether what was delivered was worth what was paid.

This is not a description of bad actors. It is a description of what systems do when feedback is absent. They drift — not toward failure, but toward whatever is most convenient for the parties operating them.

The accountability that proximity provided for free now costs money, requires infrastructure, and demands a standard to measure against. Not because anyone made it expensive. Because the scale that made the modern HOA system possible also made the natural accountability of the original model impossible to sustain.

The shift was structural. The response has to be structural too. That is what the CTI™ is.

He changed the bulb on a Thursday afternoon and walked back to his unit in a hallway that was finally, after eleven days, lit the way it should have been lit the entire time.

He did not file a complaint. He did not escalate to the board. He did not write a letter to the management company documenting the eleven days, the two calls, the person who had told him someone would follow up.

He did what most homeowners do when the system fails to respond and the cost of persistence exceeds the benefit of resolution. He absorbed the gap. He added it to the mental file of gaps he had absorbed in four years of ownership — the maintenance request that took three weeks, the annual meeting question that was acknowledged but not answered, the dues increase that arrived without the explanation that would have made it feel like something other than an imposition.

He stopped expecting the system to be organized around him. He adjusted his expectations to match the system he actually lived inside, rather than the one he had assumed existed when he signed.

That adjustment — private, invisible, absorbed without complaint — is the outcome the shift from proximity to process produces in millions of homeowners across the country every year. Not outrage. Not activism. Adaptation. The quiet recalibration of expectation that removes the feedback signal the system would need to correct itself and replaces it with the silence that allows the drift to continue.

The system did not notice when he stopped expecting it to respond. It was not organized to notice. It was organized around processing, not around the experience of the person being processed.

That is the shift. And that is what has to change.

THE ORIGIN OF THE INDUSTRY

How a homeowner-focused idea evolved into a system with different incentives — and why that matters now

The system did not begin the way it operates today. It began with a specific person, a specific conviction, and two documents that would reshape the American housing landscape for the next sixty years.

Byron Hanke was born in 1911, trained as a landscape architect at Harvard, and arrived at the Federal Housing Administration in 1945 as chief of its land planning division — a position he would hold for twenty-seven years. He was not a cabinet secretary or an agency head. He was, as one account later described him, an obscure bureaucrat in what could only be called a fourth-level position. And yet the system that governs $11 trillion in American residential wealth today runs on the framework he built.

Foundation for Community Association Research: Byron Hanke (1911–2000) was a Harvard-trained urban planner and landscape architect who served as chief of the land planning division of the FHA from 1945 to 1972.

Hanke's conviction was straightforward: homeowners who shared a roof, a road, or a reserve fund with neighbors deserved a governance structure organized around their interest. Not the developer's exit timeline. Not the management company's portfolio efficiency. Around the homeowner — the person who would live inside the consequences of every governance decision made on their behalf.

In 1963, he authored the FHA's defining publication on the subject: Planned-Unit Development with a Homes Association. The following year, his work with the Urban Land Institute produced Technical Bulletin No. 50 — The Homes Association Handbook — which became one of ULI's best-selling publications for over a decade and was distributed to more than 50,000 recipients at its release. Together, these two documents were the template. They defined how associations would be structured, how governing documents would be drafted, how authority would be distributed between the board, the management company, and the homeowners, and how the developer would transfer control when the community was complete.

CAI History: In 1964, the Urban Land Institute published Technical Bulletin No. 50: The Homes Association Handbook, the first systematic study of planned communities. The principal author was Byron Hanke. More than 50,000 copies were distributed at its release at the annual convention of the National Association of Home Builders.

What Hanke built into those documents was the assumption that proximity would do the accountability work. At the scale he was designing for — small planned communities where board members lived inside the consequences of their decisions — that assumption was correct. The governance structure he created was sound precisely because the people using it were neighbors accountable to each other in the most direct sense possible: they shared the same infrastructure, the same financial trajectory, and the same daily experience of whether the system was working.

The model worked. And because it worked, it spread. Developers adopted the template because it solved a real problem — how to maintain shared infrastructure in a community of private owners — at a cost structure the market would absorb. The FHA's mortgage insurance requirements accelerated adoption by making communities without qualifying associations ineligible for federal backing. The legal frameworks standardized across states. By the late 1960s, the HOA had become the default governance structure for new residential development across the country.

In 1963, the FHA approved federal home mortgage insurance exclusively for condominiums or for homes in subdivisions that had a qualifying HOA — a requirement that directly accelerated adoption of Hanke's template across the development industry.

What did not spread with the template was the condition that made it work.

The documents replicated. The proximity did not. A framework designed for communities of thirty-two homes was applied to communities of three hundred, then three thousand. The board member who had once lived inside every consequence of every decision now governed a community large enough that the distance between decision and outcome was measured in years. The management company that had once operated in a single building now managed portfolios of dozens. Each step was rational. Each step added a layer between the homeowner's experience and the system's accountability.

Hanke watched it happen. In 1973, he received a grant from the National Association of Home Builders to found the Community Associations Institute — the organization built to educate boards, managers, and homeowners on how to operate effectively within the system he had created. He served as its chief consultant and was its principal architect.

Foundation for Community Association Research: In 1973, Hanke received a grant from the National Association of Home Builders for $30,000 to create the Community Associations Institute and served as the chief consultant for the NAHB to design and create CAI.

By 1992, he was writing to CAI's leadership to describe what he had seen the organization become — and what it was no longer. In a letter to then-CAI president David Gibbons, Hanke and co-founder Lincoln Cummings wrote that CAI had been conceived as a research and education institute, not a lobbying or political organization, not a trade association or professional society with a narrow constituency. They wrote that CAI had quickly become dominated by those in the business — principally managers and their colleagues. They wrote that there was, and still is, little incentive for the homeowner themselves to be more than a passive observer.

Hanke and co-founder Lincoln Cummings, letter to CAI president David Gibbons, 1992: 'CAI was in part a social experiment to see if disparate interest groups could work together for the common good... CAI quickly became dominated by those in the business, principally managers and colleagues... There was, and still is, little incentive, however, for the homeowner him/herself to be more than a passive observer.'

The man who designed the system to serve homeowners lived long enough to watch the organization he founded to support that system become one that served the industry instead. He said so, in writing, in his own name, in a letter that is part of the historical record.

That is not a structural observation about drift. That is the founder of the modern HOA framework describing, from the inside, what happened to his original intent.

The goal was not to build an industry. Hanke's goal was to build a system that worked — for homeowners and for the developers creating these communities. In its early form, those interests were sufficiently aligned that the system functioned as intended. The model scaled. This was not a failure. It was a response to demand. But complexity changes incentives. As the system grew, the number of participants increased — management companies, vendors, attorneys, insurers, financial institutions — each adding value, each introducing its own incentives, none of them identical to the homeowner's.

A homeowner's interest is simple: predictable costs, stable governance, long-term value. The broader system operates on different drivers: efficiency, scale, revenue, risk management, and contract continuity. Both are rational. They are not the same. Over time, the system adapted to the incentives that sustained it — not through a single decision, not through intent, but through the accumulation of individual adjustments that each seemed minor and together changed what the system was organized to produce.

The system did not stop working. It began working differently — in ways that Hanke had specifically designed it not to work, and that the homeowners funding it had no instrument to detect.

At the state level, efforts to address these issues have not been absent. Each year, proposals are introduced to improve transparency, strengthen oversight, and rebalance homeowner interests. Hearings are held. Testimony is given. Reforms are debated. Some changes are made. Most are incremental. I have worked with legislators and leading homeowner advocates. I have sat at roundtables inside the Arizona state capitol and watched ad hoc committees form, debate, and ultimately stall or dissolve without producing meaningful structural change. In Florida, I have seen the Department of Business and Professional Regulation move decisively in response to crisis, introducing reforms and strengthening oversight. And still, the limitation remains.

You can legislate behaviors. You can require disclosures. You can adjust procedures. But you cannot, through legislation alone, fully correct a system whose underlying incentives and information flows remain unchanged. If you start at the end, it looks political. If you work backward, it looks structural. The system scaled. Incentives shifted. Visibility did not keep pace.

What has been absent is alignment between homeowner experience, system performance, and measurable accountability. Without that alignment, the system operates — but does not correct itself.

Hanke built the template with the right intent. The template was adopted without the condition that made the intent achievable. What was missing then is what is missing now — a mechanism that connects experience to accountability, that makes performance visible before its consequences arrive, that restores at scale what proximity once provided for free in communities small enough that the person making the decision was the same person living with the result.

That mechanism is what comes next.

The system Hanke designed assumed proximity would do the accountability work. At thirty-two homes, it did. At thirty thousand, it could not — and nothing was built to replace it. The template spread. The philosophy didn't. What has been missing for sixty years is not a better template. It is the instrument that makes the original intent verifiable at any scale.

CHAPTER 4

THE BUILDER'S BLUEPRINT

How the system is set before you ever arrive

The development manager's job was to get it right before anyone moved in.

He had done this eleven times. Eleven communities, across four states, over fourteen years. He knew how the process worked. He knew how to set up the governing documents, select the management company, establish the initial budget, and hand the community off to its first board in a condition that would reflect well on the builder. He was good at it. The communities he transitioned had clean records and functional operations. Nobody had ever complained about how he ran a turnover.

What he had not thought about—what the job had never asked him to think about—was what happened in year eight.

The reserve schedule he set was built on lifecycle assumptions that were standard in the industry at the time. The roofing systems were projected at twenty years. The pavement cycle was seven. The HVAC replacement window was fifteen. The monthly assessment was set at a level the market would support in a community at that price point. The reserve contribution was the residual—what was left after operational costs were covered at a fee the sales team could work with.

He moved on to the twelfth community. The eleventh community moved on without him.

Seven years later, a board member in that community pulled the original reserve study from the files and compared it to the current one. The comparison took about twenty minutes. The gap was not subtle.

The roofing systems were now thirteen years old. The reserve fund held enough to cover roughly forty percent of their projected replacement cost. The original contribution rate—set at a level the market would support—had never been adjusted to close the distance between what was being set aside and what the lifecycle actually required.

The board member brought the comparison to the next meeting. The management company representative explained that the reserve study was updated annually and that the board had always been informed of the funding percentage. The minutes from seven consecutive annual meetings confirmed this. The funding gap had been disclosed every year, in a line item on a report, in language that did not convey what a 40 percent funded reserve would eventually mean in practice.

Nobody had acted because nobody had understood what acting would have required. The disclosure had been present. The legibility had not.

The development manager had not designed a system that would fail. He had designed a system that would function—within the window he was responsible for. What happened outside that window was not part of his job description. It never had been.

THE DEVELOPMENT PROBLEM

A community governed by the HOA system begins as a development problem. The builder's objective is to deliver a product that can be financed, sold, and transitioned within a defined timeframe. That requires predictability. It requires aligning costs with what the market will accept. It requires making decisions that allow the project to move forward without introducing uncertainty that could disrupt sales or valuation.

Within those constraints, the builder creates the underlying structure of the community. Governing documents define authority and process. Financial assumptions establish the initial fee and reserve framework. Infrastructure is built with materials and systems that determine how costs will emerge over time. A management company is selected to operate the community during its early phase, and vendors are engaged to maintain it.

None of this is accidental. In larger organizations, these decisions are coordinated by people whose responsibility is to ensure that the association functions as intended once homeowners begin to occupy the space. The goal is to establish governance, select capable partners, and set the community up for success in a way that reflects well on the builder as the development progresses.

That effort is real. In the early phase it often works. The community operates coherently because design, oversight, and control are still aligned. The same group that created the system is still guiding it. The assumptions behind the financial model have not yet been tested against years of use.

The problem is not the effort. The problem is what the effort cannot see from where it stands.

A builder optimizing for delivery within a defined window is making decisions in the present about a system that will be inherited by people who are not yet there, for a lifecycle that has not yet begun. The constraints that shape those decisions—cost targets, sales pace, financing requirements, market comparables—are immediate and visible. The consequences that follow turnover are deferred and invisible.

That asymmetry is structural. It is not resolved by good intentions or careful planning. It is a feature of how development timelines and community lifecycles relate to each other. One ends. The other continues. The decisions made during the first period shape everything that happens in the second.

WHAT THE DOCUMENTS CREATE

The governing documents produced during development—the CC&Rs, bylaws, and rules—are not neutral instruments. They are frameworks written under specific conditions, by parties with specific interests, at a moment when the community does not yet exist in any meaningful sense.

The developer controls the association during the development period. That control is both necessary and consequential. It allows the project to move forward without the friction of distributed decision-making. It also means that the rules governing the community—and the financial structures embedded within them—are written before the people who will live under them have any voice in their design.

Governing documents establish how assessments are calculated, how reserves are funded, what maintenance obligations the association carries, and how authority is distributed among the board, the management company, and the homeowners. They define the baseline from which every subsequent decision is made.

In many cases, those documents are drafted using templates developed for the developer's benefit—not drafted from scratch with the specific community's long-term needs as the primary consideration. This does not make them improper. It makes them a product of the context in which they were created.

That context is worth understanding. The developer's primary obligation during the development period is to the project, not to the future community. The documents that survive into the community's operating life were written for a different purpose than the one they now serve.

THE FINANCIAL MODEL AND WHAT IT ASSUMES

The initial budget and reserve schedule are projections. They are built on assumptions about costs, inflation, component lifecycles, and usage patterns that have not yet been tested against real conditions. They are designed to be defensible and to support the sales process—which means they need to appear reasonable without introducing cost levels that the market will not accept.

Reserve funding is where this tension surfaces most clearly. Adequate reserve funding requires setting aside enough money each year to address the eventual replacement of major components—roofs, elevators, pavement, HVAC systems, pools. The amount required is determined by the age and condition of those components, their expected lifespan, and the cost of replacement when that lifespan ends.

At the point of development, most components are new. Their replacement is years or decades away. The cost of that replacement is a projection. And the reserve contribution required to fund it adequately competes directly with the monthly fee that the market will accept and the marketing materials will feature.

The result, across many communities, is an initial reserve contribution set at a level the market will support rather than a level the lifecycle requires. This is not fraud. It is optimization within constraints. But it produces a gap that compounds over time.

A community that opens with a 40 percent funded reserve trajectory does not experience that gap immediately. The components are new. The system functions. The monthly fee is within range. But as those components age, the gap between what has been set aside and what replacement will cost becomes real. By the time it surfaces—a special assessment, a deferred project, a reserve study requiring immediate action—the original financing decisions are years removed and the people responsible for them are long gone.

The board member who pulls the reserve study and runs the comparison does not see the development decision embedded in the numbers. She sees the current balance, the current trajectory, and the current gap. The origin of the condition is invisible.

THE MANAGEMENT COMPANY SELECTION

During the development period, the builder selects the management company that will operate the community. This selection happens before homeowners exist to have a preference. It is made based on the builder's operational needs, prior relationships, and the management company's ability to support the transition and early operations of the community.

That selection has consequences that extend well beyond the development period. The management company that operates a community in its first years builds institutional knowledge of the property—its systems, its vendors, its recurring issues, its board dynamics. That knowledge creates continuity, and continuity creates inertia.

Management contracts typically renew on annual terms. In practice, they persist far longer. A community that transitions out of developer control with a management company in place will often retain that company for years without a competitive evaluation. Not because the service is exceptional. Because the cost of change—the disruption, the learning curve, the relationship rebuild—creates a default toward continuation.

The management company selected during development is thus positioned, from the beginning, to become a long-term operational partner. The relationship that begins at builder selection tends to outlast the builder's involvement by a significant margin. And the accountability that should accompany that longevity—a regular, competitive evaluation against market alternatives—is rarely built into the structure the builder creates.

I have seen this directly. Communities operating with the same management company for a decade or more, where the last competitive evaluation was conducted by the developer at a time when the current board members were not yet homeowners. The contract has renewed. The fees have escalated. The service model has changed as the management company consolidated and standardized. No one has asked whether the relationship still serves the community's interests, because no one has been given a standard against which to evaluate it.

INFRASTRUCTURE AND THE LONG CYCLE

Every material choice made during construction carries a cost implication that will not surface until years later. Roofing systems with twenty-year lifespans. Pavement that requires resurfacing on a seven-year cycle. HVAC systems that perform well for fifteen years and then require systematic replacement. Pool equipment that operates within its warranty period and then begins to accumulate maintenance costs the original budget did not fully anticipate.

These choices are made within budget constraints that favor upfront cost reduction. A roofing system that costs less to install but requires replacement five years sooner than the alternative represents a genuine savings in the development budget and a genuine transfer of cost to the future community. Both of those things are true at the same time.

The homeowner who purchases a unit does not receive a disclosure explaining the expected lifecycle of the roofing system, the current reserve funding relative to that lifecycle, or the gap between the two. They receive a disclosure of the current monthly assessment and the current reserve balance. What those numbers mean in the context of what is coming is not part of the standard transaction.

Reserve studies, when conducted, are meant to close this gap. They inventory major components, estimate remaining useful life, project replacement costs, and recommend funding levels. When conducted by qualified professionals and taken seriously by the board, they provide the clearest available picture of the community's financial trajectory.

In practice, reserve studies are required in some states and voluntary in others. Where required, the standard for what constitutes an adequate study varies. Where voluntary, many communities conduct them on irregular schedules or defer the cost entirely. And in almost all cases, the reserve study is produced by a third party retained by the management company—the same party whose operational decisions have shaped the conditions the study is evaluating.

The information exists. The mechanism for producing and acting on it is inconsistent. The homeowner who depends on it to understand what she has purchased is rarely in a position to evaluate its quality.

WHAT THE INDUSTRY ALREADY KNOWS

The industry has already validated this principle externally. Lifestory Research has tracked consumer trust in home builders for fourteen years—the longest-running independent study of its kind. Their annual survey reaches tens of thousands of active home shoppers across the largest U.S. housing markets. It does not measure product quality or construction standards. It measures trust.

Taylor Morrison has held the top ranking for eleven consecutive years. That kind of sustained recognition does not come from product alone. It comes from how the buying experience is designed and delivered—from the consistency of the relationship between builder and buyer from first contact through closing.

J.D. Power measures homebuilder satisfaction on similar dimensions. Both studies point to the same conclusion: the builders who sustain recognition are the ones who treat trust as a structural commitment, not a marketing position.

The missing piece is not the buying experience. It is what happens after the builder steps away.

The trust that earned the recognition ends at closing. There is no mechanism in the governing documents that carries it forward—no requirement for independent performance measurement, no third-party accountability standard, no equivalent structure for the governance experience the homeowner lives with afterward. The system that was built to be trusted hands off to a system that has never been required to earn it.

TURNOVER AND WHAT IT TRANSFERS

At turnover, control shifts. The builder steps back, and the homeowners assume responsibility for governance. The system does not restart at that moment. It continues. What changes is who is making decisions and how those decisions are made.

Turnover is not a clean handoff. It is a transition from one form of control to another, under conditions the incoming party did not choose and often does not fully understand. The board that assumes governance at turnover inherits the governing documents, the financial structure, the management company relationship, the vendor contracts, and the reserve balance—all created during a period when they had no role in the decision-making.

In theory, the transition is supported by a process that includes financial audits, reserve study updates, condition assessments, and a structured transfer of documents and records. In practice, the quality of that process varies significantly. Some builders approach turnover as a genuine handoff, with comprehensive documentation and active support for the incoming board. Others approach it as a compliance requirement—meeting the minimum standard while minimizing the friction that a thorough process might create.

The incoming board typically has limited ability to evaluate what it has received. Its members are homeowners who volunteered to serve. They are not developers, financial analysts, or construction professionals. They are being handed responsibility for a system they did not create, with documents that reflect decisions made under different constraints and for different purposes than the ones they now face.

The management company selected during development is typically still in place at turnover. It holds the institutional knowledge of the property. It manages the vendor relationships. It produces the financial reports the board will use to understand what it has inherited. And it is, at the same moment, a party whose contract is subject to review by the board that has just assumed governance.

That relationship—between a new board that lacks institutional knowledge and a management company that holds it—is where the governance gap that will define the community's operating life is first established.

THE INTERPRETATION PROBLEM

Without a way to connect what was built to what is happening, the system tends to collapse into a single narrative. Current conditions are attributed to current actors, even when those actors are operating within constraints they did not create. Builders remain associated with the communities they developed, even though they no longer control them. Boards and management companies are held responsible for outcomes that may have roots in decisions made years before they arrived.

The system contains the answers, but not in a form anyone can see.

What is experienced can feel unpredictable. It is not. The system does not break later. It reveals itself later.

What appears to be change is often the point at which the original assumptions meet real conditions. When those conditions differ from what was modeled, adjustments follow. Fees increase, maintenance schedules shift, and financial decisions become more visible because they can no longer remain embedded in projections.

This is not a failure of intent. Builders work within constraints that require them to balance competing priorities. They optimize for delivery within a defined window.

Homeowners inherit what happens after that window closes.

That is the distinction that defines the entire structure.

WHAT CONTINUITY WOULD CHANGE

What is missing is not effort at the beginning. It is continuity between the beginning and what follows. There is no consistent way to observe how the system performs over time in relation to how it was designed. There is no standard mechanism that allows initial assumptions to be compared to actual outcomes, or that separates what was built from how it has been managed.

Without that continuity, outcomes are interpreted without context. Good performance is rarely attributed precisely. Poor performance is rarely understood in terms of how it developed. Everything compresses into what is visible in the present.

A complete system would not change how communities are built. It would make them legible over time. It would allow starting conditions to be seen alongside the outcomes they produce, creating a clearer understanding of how decisions at one stage influence results at another.

When that connection exists, the system becomes easier to understand. What once felt unpredictable becomes traceable. The focus shifts from reacting to individual outcomes to recognizing the structure that produced them.

For the builder, that visibility changes the relationship between the development period and what follows. Communities set up well—with adequate reserves, clear governance, and management relationships that serve the community's interests—perform differently over time than communities that are not. When that performance is visible, the decisions that produced it become visible too.

For the homeowner, that shift changes the nature of ownership. A home within an HOA is not just a physical asset. It is part of a system that governs how decisions are made and how money is managed over time. That system begins before the homeowner arrives and continues long after the builder has stepped away.

The development manager retired four years after the eleventh community turned over. He had completed sixteen projects in total. He was proud of the work. The communities he had set up were functioning. No one had ever called to complain.

He did not know about the board meeting in year seven. He did not know about the reserve comparison, or the funding gap, or the management company that had been in place since he selected it and had never been competitively evaluated. He did not know because there was no mechanism that would have told him. His window had closed. The system had continued without him.

The gap he had built into the reserve schedule—not out of negligence, but out of the ordinary logic of a project that needed to be financed and sold at a price the market would bear—had been compounding for seven years in a community he had not thought about since the closing documents were signed.

He had done his job correctly. The system had performed exactly as designed.

Those two things were not in conflict.

That is the point.

CHAPTER 5

WHO'S ACTUALLY IN CONTROL

The decision that reaches the board is not the decision that was made

The email did not look urgent.

It arrived late in the day, after most board members had finished their actual jobs and were moving through the end of their evenings. Three proposals attached. A recommendation included. A vote scheduled for the next meeting, two weeks out. The board members would review the attachments, compare numbers, ask questions by email, and arrive prepared to decide. The process would be documented. The vote recorded. The governance trail clean.

The outcome had already been shaped.

The proposals had been selected by the management company from vendors within its network. The comparison criteria defined by specifications it had developed. The scope of work written, in large part, by the vendor who would benefit most from a particular interpretation of what the project required. The recommendation framed around an assessment that incorporated information the board did not have and assumptions it was not positioned to evaluate.

At each step, the management company had made decisions. None were formally the board's to make. All of them shaped what the board would decide.

The board member who reviewed the email that evening was a retired teacher. She had joined the board two years ago because a neighbor had asked, and she had time, and she genuinely cared about the community she had lived in for nine years. She was not an engineer, a financial analyst, or a procurement professional. She was a neighbor who had volunteered to serve, working with the information she had been given and the time she had available after dinner on a Tuesday.

She read the three proposals. They were formatted differently but arrived at similar numbers. The management company's recommendation favored the middle option. She could not identify a reason to disagree. She approved it at the meeting two weeks later, along with four other board members who had reached the same conclusion.

The project was completed. The work was adequate. The cost was $100,000 above what a competitive bid process would have produced.

Nobody knew that. There was no mechanism by which anyone would have known it. The benchmark that would have told the board what comparable communities paid for equivalent work had never been constructed. The board had approved a reasonable-seeming number in the absence of any standard against which reasonable could be defined.

That is not a failure of intent. It is a failure of information. And information failures, at the scale of 40 million homes and $140 billion in annual dues, are not small.

WHERE AUTHORITY LIVES AND WHERE CONTROL LIVES

There is a distinction at the center of HOA governance that most homeowners never encounter and most board members never fully examine. It is the distinction between authority and control.

Authority sits with the board. The board has the legal power to make decisions about the community's finances, maintenance, enforcement, and vendor relationships. It is elected by homeowners to exercise that authority in their interest. Its decisions are documented, its meetings are theoretically open, its votes are recorded.

Control sits somewhere else entirely.

Control sits where options are created. Where the scope of work is written. Where the vendor list is assembled. Where comparison criteria are defined. Where the recommendation is framed. Where the information the board will use to make its decision is organized, filtered, and presented by the party that organized, filtered, and presented it.

In the modern HOA system, that party is almost always the management company.

The management company does not govern. It executes. But execution—when it includes defining what is to be executed and organizing the information that governs the decision to execute it—looks, from the homeowner's perspective, indistinguishable from governance. The board approves. The management company defines what is approved. Authority and control are located in different places, exercised by different parties, accountable to different things.

The board governs the information it receives. The question nobody asks is who decided what information to provide.

Understanding this distinction explains why communities governed by engaged, well-intentioned boards can still produce outcomes that homeowners experience as unresponsive, expensive, and disconnected from their interests. The board members are not the problem. In most communities, they are neighbors who volunteered to serve—attending meetings they are not paid to attend, reviewing documents they were not trained to evaluate, making decisions based on information provided by people with more expertise than they have.

The expertise gap is not an accident. It is a structural feature of how the modern HOA operates. Management companies are professional organizations staffed by people who spend their careers inside this system. Board members are volunteers who entered when elected and will leave when their term ends. The gap is wide, persistent, and rarely acknowledged by either party.

In a well-functioning relationship, that expertise serves the community. The management company brings professional knowledge to decisions volunteer board members could not be expected to make without it. The board brings the homeowner perspective that keeps professional expertise anchored to the community's actual needs. The productive tension between them is what governance looks like.

The problem emerges when the expertise gap grows large enough that the board cannot effectively evaluate the options it receives. At that point, approval becomes a formality. The governance trail is clean, but governance itself has become largely ceremonial—a process whose outcome was determined before the vote.

HOW DECISIONS ARE ACTUALLY MADE

A vendor is selected. The homeowner who receives the work does not know how that vendor was chosen, what alternatives were considered, or what relationships existed between the selecting party and the selected vendor before the contract was signed.

A maintenance schedule is set. The homeowner who pays dues to support it does not know what drove the timing decisions, what tradeoffs were made between immediate cost and long-term condition, or what difference the chosen schedule makes against alternatives that were not.

A reserve contribution rate is established. The homeowner who will absorb the difference between adequate and inadequate funding does not know what assumptions drove the rate or what the reserve fund's trajectory looks like at the rate chosen.

In each case, a decision was made with real consequences for the homeowner's financial exposure and daily experience. The homeowner did not make it. The board approved a version of it that had already been shaped. The management company organized the information that shaped that approval. The vendor, the management company, and the board each operated within its own frame—while the homeowner funded everything and understood the least.

THE BOARD THAT DOESN'T KNOW WHAT IT DOESN'T KNOW

The most consequential governance failures in the HOA system are not the ones where the board knew what was happening and chose to allow it. The dramatic failures—misappropriated funds, fraudulent management companies and boards, vendors who performed work never completed—are real and harmful, but they are not the primary source of the $28 billion in annual waste the absence of accountability has sustained.

The primary source is something quieter.

The board that didn't know what it didn't know. That evaluated its management company using reports the management company produced. That reviewed vendor bids solicited by the management company from vendors the management company selected. That governed entirely within the information environment the party being governed had organized.

At each step, the board was operating one layer of abstraction above the decisions that mattered. It was approving outputs it had not generated, using frameworks it had not designed, based on expertise it did not have, in a time window that rarely allowed for independent verification.

The board member who could not identify a reason to disagree was not failing her community. She was doing exactly what the system was designed to ask of her.

The problem is not that she approved without independent verification. The problem is that the system was designed to ask her to approve without it—and that the absence of an external standard meant there was nothing against which the recommendation could be checked.

She was governing the information she received. Carefully. With genuine intent. What she could not do was govern the information she did not receive, or evaluate the recommendation against a benchmark that did not exist.

That is the governance gap. Not a failure of character or commitment. A failure of the information environment in which governance takes place.

THE THREE DECISIONS NOBODY SEES

To understand where control actually lives in the modern HOA, trace three decisions from origin to outcome. Each shapes the homeowner's financial exposure and daily experience. Each is made, in whole or in part, before it reaches the board.

The first is vendor selection. The board typically receives bids solicited by the management company from a list it maintains. That list is not a neutral market roster. It is a managed network—shaped by relationships, referral arrangements, and internal preferences.

The board choosing from that list is not choosing from the market. It is choosing from the management company's representation of the market.

In some cases, that representation includes firms that appear independent but are not. Ownership overlaps. Control overlaps. The same decision-making influence sits behind multiple proposals presented as separate options.

I have seen this structure directly—a board requesting three bids for a management contract and receiving the incumbent alongside two alternatives, one of which was owned and controlled by the same party. The requirement for competition had been met on paper. The outcome had not changed.

The appearance of competition is present. The structure of competition is not.

The second is scope definition. The scope of work is often written by parties with an interest in the outcome. The board approving that scope is ratifying a definition it did not create.

The third is performance evaluation. When work is complete, the evaluation is typically performed by the same party that selected the vendor and defined the work. This is not independent evaluation. It is self-assessment with structure.

Three decisions. All consequential. None fully visible to the board formally responsible for governance. Each made by the party that knows the most and is accountable to the least.

WHAT THE HOMEOWNER FUNDS WITHOUT KNOWING

The homeowner who pays $450 a month is funding the decisions described above. The vendor selected from a preferred network rather than a competitive market. The scope written to match the available budget rather than the work the property required. The evaluation that reported satisfactory performance because the evaluator arranged the work.

She is not funding these decisions knowingly. She is funding a line item called "maintenance" that reflects the accumulated outcome of decisions she had no part in making and no instrument for evaluating.

This is the structural condition of the modern HOA—a system in which the parties responsible for execution have more information than the parties responsible for governance, and the parties responsible for governance have more authority than the parties most affected by the decisions.

The homeowner, who is most affected, has the least authority and the least information.

That arrangement has produced $28 billion in annual waste. Not through malice. Through the ordinary operation of a system that has never been required to produce a verified, external, homeowner-derived account of whether what it is doing matches what the people funding it would choose if they could see it.

WHAT CHANGES WHEN PERFORMANCE IS MEASURED

The board that knows its governance quality is being measured by the people it governs is in a fundamentally different information environment than the board that is not.

Not because the board members are suddenly more capable. Not because the management company has changed its practices. What changes is the reference point.

The CTI™ score on the community's public page is not mediated by the management company. It is not produced by the board. It reflects the direct, verified experience of the homeowners who live inside the decisions the board has been making—homeowners whose maintenance requests have or have not been resolved, whose financial communications have or have not been comprehensible, whose questions have or have not been answered.

That signal is what proximity once provided for free. The board member who lived inside the consequences of her decisions knew, without being told, whether the homeowners around her were satisfied. She could see it. She could not avoid it.

The CTI™ gives the modern board what proximity once made inevitable: a direct, unmediated account of how governance translates into the daily experience of the people being governed. Not filtered through a management company report. Organized around the homeowner's experience—because that is the only frame that matters when the question is whether the community is being governed in their interest.

When the board knows it is being measured, it governs differently. Not because external measurement transforms character. Because external measurement provides the reference point that character alone cannot create.

The board that sees a 2.6 governance score against a market average of 4.1 knows something it did not know before. Not that it has failed—scores can be improved. That the decisions it has been making, as experienced by verified homeowners who live with their consequences, are producing an outcome that comparable communities are not producing.

That information is the beginning of accountability. For fifty years, it did not exist in a form the board could use.

It does now.

THE RETIRED TEACHER WHO CHANGED HER VOTE

She voted to approve the proposal two weeks after the email arrived, along with the rest of the board. The project was completed. She walked past the results on her way to the parking lot. They looked fine.

Eight months later, the community joined the CTI™ platform. She received the first quarterly report. She saw the composite score. She saw the dimension breakdown. She saw the market comparison showing comparable communities in her zip code spending significantly less for equivalent maintenance outcomes.

She did not immediately understand why.

She opened the maintenance execution section. She read the homeowner narratives. Six of the twelve open-text comments described the same pattern: vendor work requiring follow-up visits, extended response times since the last contract renewal, a gap between what was reported as completed and what homeowners described as actually resolved.

She set the report down. She picked up the phone and called the board chair.

Not because she had discovered fraud. Because she had discovered, for the first time, the distance between what the management company's reports described and what the verified homeowners in her community were experiencing.

That distance had always been there. She had simply never had an instrument to see it.

The instrument existed now. And what it revealed was the beginning of a conversation the system had never been designed to have.

CHAPTER 6

THE MANAGEMENT LAYER IS CHANGING

What consolidation produced–and what it costs the homeowner who never saw it happen

The name on the management company's letterhead changed.

She had lived in the community for nine years and had learned, the way long-term residents learn things, which details mattered and which didn't. The name on the letterhead was not one of them. Companies changed names. They got acquired. They rebranded. It was one item in a stack of correspondence that required no action and received none.

What she did not know—what there was no mechanism for her to know—was that the name change represented something more consequential than a rebrand. The management company that had held her community's contract for seven years had been acquired by a regional platform that had itself been acquired, eighteen months earlier, by a national firm managing more than three thousand communities across fourteen states.

The manager who had answered calls personally—who knew the community's history, its recurring maintenance issues, its board dynamics, the particular challenges of the parking structure that flooded in heavy rain—had been reassigned. She was now responsible for six additional communities. The contract her company held with the association did not meaningfully change.

Her replacement was newer to the portfolio, handling a larger load, operating from a centralized service platform designed to standardize interactions across hundreds of associations simultaneously.

The structure had changed. The price had not. What the community was paying for had shifted. No one had been asked to evaluate the change.

I have seen this structure directly—managers spread across too many communities to maintain real knowledge of any one of them, while the cost to the community remained effectively the same. The service model scaled. The accountability did not.

The community's average request response time extended from three days to twelve. The financial reports changed format—cleaner in some ways, less contextual in others, optimized for the platform's reporting requirements rather than the board's understanding of what the numbers meant. The vendor relationships built over years gave way to the platform's preferred network, offering consistency across the portfolio at prices reflecting purchasing arrangements rather than the local market.

None of this was announced.

It happened in the background, the way structural changes in systems almost always happen—through the accumulation of individual adjustments that each seemed minor and, together, changed the nature of the service the community was receiving.

She noticed something had changed. She could not have told you precisely what. The building felt different. More institutional. Less like a community being tended to by someone with a stake in its condition and more like a property being processed by a system with a portfolio to manage.

The feeling was real. The mechanism producing it was invisible.

THE INDUSTRY THAT CONSOLIDATED WHILE NOBODY WAS WATCHING

The professional property management industry underwent significant consolidation beginning in the early 2000s and accelerating through the following two decades. Regional firms built on local relationships and community knowledge were acquired by national platforms offering technology infrastructure, standardized processes, and the operational efficiency that comes from managing at scale.

The consolidation was rational from an investment perspective. Property management is a volume business. Margins on any single community contract are thin—typically measured in the low hundreds of dollars per unit per year. Profitability requires managing many communities efficiently, not a few exceptionally well. The firms that grew figured out how to lower the per-community cost of service delivery—standardizing service, centralizing back-office functions, building technology that allowed fewer managers to handle more communities.

Private equity accelerated the process. The industry's recurring revenue model—contracts that renewed annually, dues that arrived monthly, portfolios that grew through acquisition—was attractive to investors seeking predictable cash flows. Capital that entered through the 2010s funded the acquisitions that consolidated regional firms into national platforms.

From the investment perspective, consolidation created value. From the homeowner's perspective, the question it raised has never been clearly answered: did service quality improve, decline, or change in ways that made it harder to evaluate?

The honest answer is that it changed in ways that made it harder to evaluate. And harder to evaluate, in a system with no external performance standard, has functioned as a proxy for fine.

WHAT DISTANCE COSTS

Distance in property management is not measured in miles. It is measured in the number of communities a single manager carries, the depth of knowledge about any single community's history, the average time between a homeowner's request and a human response, and the speed at which problems are identified before they compound into concentrated cost events.

A manager who knows a community—who understands that the elevator in Building C has a recurring winter issue requiring an adjustment rather than a standard service call, that the homeowner in Unit 412 needs resolution rather than another acknowledgment, that the finance committee chair will want the reserve study reviewed before any capital expenditure is approved—produces different outcomes than a manager working from a ticketing system across a portfolio too large for that kind of knowledge to exist.

Neither manager is necessarily failing to do their job. The first is doing community management. The second is doing portfolio administration. The homeowner experiences the difference regardless of how the job is defined.

The maintenance request that takes three days in a managed-for-knowledge system takes twelve in a managed-for-efficiency system. The financial report that arrives with context in one arrives as a formatted table without context in the other. Each difference is individually tolerable. Together, over time, they produce the degradation of homeowner experience that the CTI™ maintenance execution and communication dimensions are built to surface—the pattern invisible in any single interaction and unmistakable across twelve months of verified homeowner accounts.

THE STANDARDIZATION THAT REPLACES KNOWLEDGE

When management companies scale to the point where institutional knowledge of individual communities becomes impractical to maintain, they replace knowledge with process. This is not a cynical choice. It is a structural one. Process is the only thing that scales across hundreds of communities simultaneously. Knowledge, by definition, cannot be standardized—it is specific, contextual, and built through time spent inside a particular system.

Standardized templates replace personal responses. Automated ticketing replaces the manager who knew which vendor to call for which issue. Centralized vendor rosters replace local procurement that produced genuine price competition. Compliance monitoring systems that flag violations across a portfolio replace the manager who knew which homeowners had ongoing situations requiring something other than a standard notice.

Process is not knowledge. It is a substitute for knowledge that is cheaper to deploy at scale. And cheaper-at-scale, in a system with no external performance standard, tends to become the standard.

The homeowner who submits a maintenance request and receives an automated acknowledgment followed by a form-letter update three weeks later is experiencing standardization. The homeowner who calls a manager who knows their building—and gets a timeline from someone who knows the vendor, the issue, and the history—is experiencing knowledge. The CTI™ communication dimension measures the gap between them because the homeowners living in that gap know it precisely, and their verified account of it is the signal the market needs to distinguish between the two.

THE MANAGER IN THE MIDDLE

It would be a mistake to read this chapter as an indictment of individual property managers working inside the consolidated platforms. This is not a story of people who chose to deliver worse service. It is a story of people whose jobs were changed around them by structural forces they did not control, doing those jobs with genuine professionalism inside systems that make genuine community knowledge increasingly difficult to maintain.

The manager who handles thirty communities is not lazy. She is overextended. The system that assigned her thirty communities made a calculation about the acceptable ratio of manager capacity to portfolio size—a calculation made by people whose primary frame was operational efficiency rather than service quality. She inherited the result.

She processes maintenance requests for thirty communities through a centralized platform. She communicates using platform templates. She attends board meetings for thirty communities per quarter and presents reports the platform generates. She does all of this competently and professionally, at a pace that leaves her approximately three minutes of community attention per community per day.

Three minutes per community per day is not community management. It is triage.

The best managers inside the consolidated platforms do more than their systems require. They develop genuine knowledge of the communities they serve, maintain it despite structural obstacles, and deliver service quality the platform's metrics would not predict. They exist. They matter. And they are working against a structure that makes their excellence the exception rather than the expectation.

What the CTI™ individual manager performance record provides is something no prior system has offered: a verified, portable, public record of the service quality they deliver—visible to every board evaluating a management contract. The manager whose scores are consistently above the market benchmark across every community she has served has always existed. What she has never had is the instrument to prove it. The CTI™ gives her that instrument—and in doing so, creates the career incentive for management professionals to pursue genuine community knowledge rather than portfolio size.

THE HOMEOWNER WHO PAYS THE DIFFERENCE

The cost of the management layer's transformation is not abstract. It is measured in deferred maintenance a knowledgeable manager would have caught before it compounded. In vendor contracts priced above market because standardization removed the local competition that would have benchmarked them. In special assessments that represent, in part, the accumulated cost of governance that was technically delivered but operationally thin for long enough that the thinness became unavoidable.

The homeowner paying $450 a month to a management company operating her community from a centralized platform across a portfolio of forty-three is paying for a service that was redesigned—without her knowledge or consent—to serve the management company's operational model rather than her community's needs. The contract looks the same. The monthly fee is the same. The service reflects a fundamental change in what the system was organized to produce.

This is structure. Not accusation. The management companies that consolidated did not do so with the intent to reduce service quality. Most genuinely believe their standardized platforms deliver better, more consistent service than the fragmented local operations they replaced. They may be right about consistency. They are not always right about quality. And the difference between those two things is precisely what the CTI™ is built to measure.

When performance is visible—when the management company's execution score is derived from the verified accounts of homeowners inside the communities it manages, compared against the market benchmark for communities of comparable type and size—the company that delivers genuine service quality has a competitive advantage it can demonstrate. The company that delivers process without quality has nowhere to hide.

That visibility changes the incentive structure of the entire industry. Not immediately. Not without friction. But in the direction markets always move when performance becomes measurable: toward the quality the signal rewards.

THE HOMEOWNER WHO FINALLY FILED A COMPLAINT

She filed a complaint six months after the name on the letterhead changed. Not a dramatic complaint—a specific one. The parking structure drainage issue that had been on the deferred maintenance list for three years had been escalated at the last board meeting, assigned to a vendor, and then gone silent. The vendor had visited. A report had been filed. No work had been scheduled. The rainy season was six weeks away.

She submitted through the platform's online portal. An automated acknowledgment arrived within four hours. Three weeks later, with no follow-up, she called. The person who answered could access the ticket but could not tell her what had happened to the vendor report or when work would be scheduled. They would follow up.

They did not follow up.

She raised it at the next board meeting. The representative attending that evening—covering for her community's assigned manager, who had a conflict—looked up the ticket and reported it was marked as pending vendor scheduling. She asked when. He said he would follow up.

The rainy season arrived. The parking structure flooded. The repair that could have been completed for $14,000 in the summer became an emergency remediation that cost $67,000 in November.

The management company had not failed in any way its contract defined as failure. The ticket had been logged. The vendor had been notified. The platform had operated as designed. The outcome that operation produced was not the platform's problem.

It was the communities.

That outcome—and the verified homeowner account of the sequence that produced it—is now on the community's CTI™ page. Permanent. Visible to every board evaluating a management contract, every buyer considering a unit, every lender underwriting a loan.

The management layer changed. The homeowner paid for the change. The market is now learning to see the cost.

CHAPTER 7

WHERE INCENTIVES TAKE OVER

Where the money actually flows and why the system aligns accordingly

The contract was approved on a Tuesday evening in March.

The board had reviewed three proposals. The management company had solicited them, organized them into a comparison document, and provided a recommendation. The numbers were in the same general range. The recommended vendor had a relationship with the management company that predated the community's contract by several years. None of that was visible in the comparison document. None of it was required to be.

The board voted four to one in favor of the recommendation. The dissenting vote came from a board member who had wanted to solicit additional bids from outside the management company's network. She was outvoted. The contract was signed. The work was completed on schedule. The vendor performed adequately.

Another transaction occurred beneath it.

Invisible.

The management company received a referral fee from the vendor—a standard arrangement within its preferred network, disclosed in the management contract in language that described the practice in general terms without specifying amounts, frequency, or the list of vendors to which it applied. The board had signed the management contract. The disclosure was in the contract. The board had approved what it was told it was approving.

I have seen management contracts that require a 10 percent marketing fee on all vendor referrals. The particular contract I am thinking of also included a confidentiality clause—one that required the vendor not to disclose the fee to board members or homeowners. The arrangement had been disclosed to the board in the management contract. The terms of that arrangement had been contractually concealed from the board by the same document.

The homeowner paid once. The system benefited twice. And the mechanism that made that possible had been written into the paperwork they signed.

The dissenting board member raised the referral arrangement at the next meeting. She had found the disclosure language and had questions about how it applied to the contract they had just approved. The board president said the arrangement was standard industry practice and had been disclosed. The management company representative confirmed it. The meeting moved on.

She did not raise it again. Not because she was satisfied with the answer. Because she understood, in the way people understand things they cannot prove, that raising it further would cost her—social capital, goodwill, the working relationship with the board chair that made the rest of her service functional—while any benefit would be shared across every homeowner in the community.

She absorbed the information. She filed it away. She continued to serve.

The system continued to operate.

HOW INCENTIVES SHAPE SYSTEMS

This is structure. Not accusation.

Every system involving multiple parties, layered relationships, and money flowing in multiple directions will develop incentive structures. Those structures are not designed by any single actor to produce any particular outcome. They emerge from the decisions each party makes in its own interest, within the constraints of the system it operates inside, over time.

Incentive structures shape behavior. Behavior produces outcomes. Outcomes accumulate into the daily experience of the people the system is meant to serve.

The HOA system is not unusual in having incentive structures that do not always align with homeowner interests. Every complex service industry has them. The question is not whether they exist. The question is whether they are visible—and whether the people whose money funds them have the information required to evaluate whether they are getting value.

In most cases, HOA homeowners are not getting that information. Not because it is being concealed in any formal sense. Because the system was organized, long before any individual homeowner arrived inside it, around the interests of the parties with the most power to shape it. Systems organized that way tend to remain that way until something external forces the reckoning.

The CTI™ is that something external.

WHERE THE MONEY FLOWS

The dues a homeowner pays each month enter a financial system more complex than most homeowners understand and more consequential than most boards fully see.

A portion funds direct community expenses: landscaping, utilities, insurance premiums, administrative costs—the visible layer that produces observable outcomes.

Another portion funds the management contract—the monthly fee paid for operational services. This number appears in the budget. It is approved by the board. It is where most conversations about cost begin and end.

What is not visible is the structure that sits beneath it.

The management contract does not exist in isolation. It creates an ecosystem of additional revenue streams that are rarely understood in full.

Vendor referral arrangements are one layer. Compensation for directing community business toward preferred vendors may take the form of direct referral fees, marketing fees tied to promotion of services, volume-based incentives, or reciprocal relationships that provide value across a broader network. I have seen agreements where these arrangements were disclosed in form but not in substance—referenced generally, without detail on amounts, counterparties, or frequency.

These structures are often legal with appropriate disclosure. They are also, by design, positioned alongside the procurement process they influence.

Technology platform fees are another layer. They appear in the budget as operational expenses, but reflect a cost structure that serves both the community's administrative needs and the management company's ability to scale efficiently across its portfolio.

Ancillary service fees add further depth. Maintenance coordination. Violation processing. Document preparation. Each individually small. Together, meaningful.

None of these mechanisms are inherently improper.

But disclosure is not visibility.

A contract that notes, in general language, that compensation "may be received" is not the same as a clear accounting of how much was received, from whom, and tied to which decisions.

The homeowner who reads the disclosure has been informed. They have not been shown.

And in a system where behavior only changes when it is visible, being informed is not enough.

INCENTIVES FOLLOW VISIBILITY

Where visibility is absent, incentives follow themselves.

The management company that benefits from directing work toward a preferred network has an incentive to do exactly that. No malice required. No coordination required. Only the ordinary behavior of an organization operating without external constraint.

The board that approves those contracts without the ability to benchmark them is not complicit. It is operating without the information required to evaluate them.

The vendor that wins work through relationship rather than competition has no incentive to price competitively. The competitive mechanism that would enforce discipline has been removed before the decision reaches the board.

The homeowner absorbs the outcome at the end of this chain without the ability to trace it back to its source.

The dues increase is attributed to rising costs. The special assessment is attributed to deferred maintenance. Both are true.

Neither identifies the procurement structure that contributed to both—year after year, through decisions that appeared reasonable in isolation and were never measured against an external reference point.

Each participant is behaving rationally within its own incentives. No single actor needs to act improperly for the outcome to emerge.

This is what systems do in the absence of visibility. They optimize for the parties with the most ability to shape them.

THE COST OF OPACITY

Procurement opacity does not produce obviously bad outcomes.

Preferred vendors are typically qualified. The work is typically adequate. The pricing is typically defensible within the context it is presented.

The problem is not the work. The problem is the absence of a benchmark.

A community that pays $85,000 for a project that could have been completed for $62,000 has not been defrauded. The work was completed. The process was followed. The outcome was simply more expensive than it needed to be.

That difference is real money.

It is paid by homeowners who will later be told that costs are rising due to inflation, market pressure, or aging infrastructure.

Those factors are real. The structural conditions that removed the competitive pressure that would have moderated them are not part of the explanation.

At scale, these differences compound.

Across billions in annual HOA spend, the cumulative effect is not marginal. It is material.

The $28 billion in annual waste does not primarily live in fraud. It lives in the ordinary operation of a system that presents the appearance of competition without consistently producing it—and that has never been required to demonstrate the difference.

That is the cost of opacity.

Riva on the River Homeowners Association v. The Management Association, Inc. d/b/a The Management Trust, filed in the Eastern District of California, is still being litigated. No court has determined liability. But the allegations go directly to the question this chapter is asking: where does the money flow, who benefits from it, and what did the client actually understand?

At issue are payments allegedly connected to HOA client funds placed with banks. Public summaries of the class-certification materials describe a distinction that matters: the payments are not being characterized as traditional earnings credits. They are being described as cash payments to management companies connected to the placement of client deposits. The alleged payments exceed $33 million over a class period beginning in 2012.

I am not an attorney. I am not making a legal conclusion. The court will decide what happened in that case. But structurally, the concern is clear: when money belonging to an association produces a benefit for the party managing that money, disclosure alone may not be enough.

Was the benefit clearly disclosed? Was it understood by the association? Was it tied to money that belonged to the client? Did the client have a meaningful choice in where that money was placed?

The homeowner has been informed. They have not necessarily been shown.

That is the danger of opacity. It does not merely conceal a number. It collapses the distinction between the manager who followed the system and the executive who designed it—between the board that never saw the arrangement and the homeowner whose funds generated the benefit.

Eventually, someone asks the right question.

And when they do, the issue is no longer whether the practice was common.

It is whether it should have been visible all along.

THE RESERVE FUND THAT SHRINKS WITHOUT A DECISION

Procurement opacity is the most visible expression of misaligned incentives in the HOA system. It is not the only one.

The reserve fund that declines gradually over years without any single decision to decline it reflects a different misalignment—one that operates at the board level and involves no financial arrangement that can be pointed to.

Board members are elected by homeowners. Homeowners generally prefer lower dues. The board member who delivers dues stability gets re-elected. The one who recommends a dues increase to achieve adequate reserve funding faces a harder conversation at the annual meeting.

This is not a conspiracy. It is a rational response to an incentive structure. What homeowners want, expressed consistently through the political dynamics of the annual meeting, is dues stability. What the community needs, expressed clearly through the reserve study that most homeowners never read, is adequate reserve funding.

The result is the reserve fund that is technically disclosed, annually reviewed, and consistently underfunded—because the incentive structure of the system produces underfunding as its natural output in the absence of external accountability.

WHAT CHANGES WHEN PERFORMANCE IS VISIBLE

The management company whose performance is measured against a verified homeowner signal it cannot control has a different incentive structure than one that operates without measurement.

The CTI™ maintenance execution score does not audit procurement practices or show what referral fees were earned on which transactions. It shows something more directly consequential: whether homeowners experience their maintenance as well-managed, responsive, and reliable.

If the preferred vendor model produces genuinely good outcomes—qualified contractors, responsive service, work homeowners experience as satisfactory—the score will reflect that. The management company that delivers genuine quality through its preferred vendor network has nothing to fear from visibility.

If the preferred vendor model produces cost without quality—adequate work, slow delivery, above-market prices, indifferent service—the score will reflect that too. The management company whose scores are consistently below the market benchmark across its portfolio now has a problem its preferred vendor relationships cannot solve.

The referral arrangement invisible in the management contract is now visible in its outcome. The procurement opacity that removed the competitive process is now visible in the score it produces for the homeowners who live with the result.

Incentives follow visibility. The management company that cannot hide below-benchmark performance has an incentive to improve it. The board that can see its governance score against the market average has an incentive to close the gap. The vendor whose work is described by the homeowners who live with it has an incentive to deliver work worth describing positively.

None of this requires a regulator or a mandate. It requires the verified signal that makes performance visible—and a market that, once it can see performance, chooses quality over opacity.

THE DISSENTING BOARD MEMBER

She served for three more years after the meeting where she raised the referral arrangement and was outvoted. She voted against two more management company recommendations she could not independently verify. She was outvoted both times.

In her final year of service, the community joined the CTI™ platform. She attended the board meeting where the first quarterly report was presented. She watched the board chair review the maintenance execution score—below the market benchmark for three consecutive quarters—and listened to the management company representative explain that the scores reflected a small number of dissatisfied homeowners and should not be taken as indicative of overall service quality.

She asked a question she had not been able to ask before.

She asked: what does the market benchmark represent, and which communities are producing it?

The answer was specific. The benchmark represented the average CTI™ maintenance execution score across comparable communities in the same market—communities of the same type, size, and governance structure, managed by a range of management companies, producing outcomes verified by the homeowners inside them.

She asked a second question.

She asked: if comparable communities are consistently scoring above us on maintenance, what is different about how they are procuring and managing that work?

Nobody in the room had an answer. But the question had been asked, on the record, at a board meeting, in a community that now had a verified performance signal against which the management company's answer would eventually have to be measured.

The incentive structure had not changed. The visibility had.

In a system where incentives follow visibility, that is where change begins.

CHAPTER 8

THE INVISIBLE RISKS

The costs that were building the entire time–and the structure that kept them that way

The roof was fourteen years old.

The reserve study from three years prior had estimated its remaining useful life at eight to twelve years. That study had been conducted by a licensed professional, reviewed by the board at the annual meeting where it was presented, and filed with the association's records. It was available to any homeowner who asked for it. The process had been followed. The document existed.

None of the homeowners in the building had asked for it. Not because they were careless. Because there was no reason to look. The roof did not appear to be failing. There were no visible leaks in the common areas, no staining on the hallway ceilings, no signs that anything was deteriorating beyond the ordinary aging every building shows over fourteen years. The community looked fine. The building functioned. The dues were paid.

Then the rains came harder than usual over a three-day period in late October, and three units on the top floor reported water intrusion the same week. The board authorized an emergency inspection. The inspector found not three problem areas but eleven. The substrate beneath the membrane in two sections had been compromised for what appeared to be eighteen months to two years. The membrane itself had reached the end of its useful life in several locations simultaneously.

Within a month, an emergency assessment had been called. Within two months, a number had been assigned to each unit owner.

Special Assessment: $14,500. Per unit.

The roof had not failed without warning. The warning had never been organized into a picture the homeowners who needed it could use before the consequence arrived. The reserve study had predicted the failure window. The contribution rate had not been adjusted to match it. The maintenance that might have extended the roof's useful life had been performed on a schedule that reflected budget constraints rather than condition monitoring.

The biggest costs in HOA living are not the ones you see coming. They are the ones that were building the entire time.

HOW BREAKDOWNS HAPPEN

Most breakdowns in HOA communities do not originate from a single decision. They develop over time, through the accumulation of small gaps that individually seem manageable and collectively produce something that none of them, viewed alone, would have suggested.

Delayed maintenance that was not fully tracked. Financial assumptions that were not revisited when conditions changed. Vendor decisions made without consistent benchmarking. Information that existed in fragments but was never assembled into a comprehensive picture.

None of these gaps are unusual on their own. What makes the HOA system distinctive is the combination of volunteer governance, professional execution, and distributed accountability that makes it structurally difficult for any single participant to see the full picture. The board sees what the management company presents. The management company sees what its systems capture. The vendor sees the scope of work it was assigned. The homeowner sees the outcome.

By the time the outcome is visible, the sequence that produced it is buried in years of incremental decisions that each seemed reasonable in the moment they were made.

The question that matters is not who to blame. It is what structure made the sequence possible and what signal could have made it visible early enough to change it.

WHAT MAKES A RISK INVISIBLE

The risks described in this chapter are not hidden in any meaningful sense. They are documented. They exist in reserve studies, in maintenance logs, in insurance certificates, in financial statements that the management company produces and the board approves and the homeowners receive without the context required to interpret them.

What makes them invisible is not concealment. It is the absence of the mechanism that turns available information into usable signal at the moment when the person who needs it can act on it.

The reserve study that predicts a roof failure in eight to twelve years is accessible to any homeowner who knows to request it and understands how to interpret it. What is missing is the layer that translates that prediction into plain language before the annual meeting where the contribution rate will be set. Something that says: the reserve study projects roof replacement within four to six years. The current contribution rate funds approximately 60 percent of that cost. If the rate is not adjusted, the gap will arrive as a special assessment.

That communication does not require sophisticated technology. It requires a governance culture that treats homeowners as the customers the system exists to serve rather than the compliance subjects it is designed to manage. And that governance culture—as the emotional trust dimension of the CTI™ measures in community after community—is precisely what the system operating without external accountability has most consistently failed to produce.

THE SPECIAL ASSESSMENT THAT WASN'T SUDDEN

For many homeowners, nothing creates more financial disruption than a special assessment that arrives without warning. The amount can be significant—tens of thousands of dollars per unit. The timing is rarely convenient. The explanation offered rarely connects the number to the decisions that produced it.

From the outside, it looks like failure. From inside the system that produced it, it looks like the predictable outcome of a sequence documented and discussed and deferred across years of governance that prioritized dues stability over reserve adequacy.

The sequence is consistent. Reserve contributions fall behind long-term needs—not dramatically, not in any single year that would produce alarm, but consistently, year after year, by small amounts that accumulate into a significant gap. Maintenance is deferred without adequate tracking of what the accumulation represents as a future cost. Cost projections fail to account for the inflation affecting construction and labor at rates that historical reserve studies did not anticipate.

By the time a major repair becomes unavoidable, the funding gap is already established. The gap becomes the assessment. The assessment feels sudden.

It was not.

The CTI™ financial stewardship dimension is the instrument that makes the trajectory visible before it becomes the assessment. Not by replacing the reserve study—the reserve study remains the authoritative document for reserve planning. By measuring whether homeowners experience their board as proactively planning for future capital needs or managing dues for short-term stability. That distinction, expressed in the verified accounts of people who attend the annual meetings and receive the financial reports and watch the contribution rate hold steady for the fourth consecutive year, is the leading indicator that the reserve study's trajectory is not translating into governance action.

INSURANCE INSTABILITY

Insurance has become one of the most volatile cost drivers in HOA communities over the past five years, and it operates almost entirely outside the visibility that homeowners have into how their community is being managed.

The dynamics are well documented at a market level. Carriers in the country's largest HOA states—Florida, Texas, California—have repriced coastal and wildfire risk at levels that HOA budgets were never designed to absorb. Some carriers have exited those markets entirely, leaving communities scrambling for replacement coverage at costs that represent multiples of prior premiums. The communities that were watching—that had governance structures reviewing insurance coverage annually against market conditions, that maintained adequate reserves to absorb premium increases without assessment—were prepared for the disruption. The ones that were not found out when the renewal arrived.

Insurance instability is not only a coastal or wildfire-zone problem. It is a governance problem wherever insurance coverage is treated as a fixed-cost assumption rather than an active management responsibility.

Coverage terms change at renewal. Exclusions expand. Deductibles increase. Sub-limits shift. The policy that covered a loss two years ago may not cover it today.

The risk lives in the gap between what the homeowner assumes is covered and what the current policy actually covers. That gap is tested only at the moment of claim—when the loss has occurred, the damage is real, and the coverage expected to respond does not respond in the way the homeowner believed it would.

The CTI™ financial stewardship dimension measures homeowner experience of how proactively the board communicates on financial matters, including insurance. The community whose homeowners consistently describe insurance coverage as clearly communicated, regularly reviewed, and proactively managed is a community whose board is treating insurance as the active governance responsibility it has become.

DEFERRED MAINTENANCE COMPOUNDING

Deferred maintenance is the most common source of concentrated cost events in HOA communities. It is also the risk most clearly visible in retrospect and most consistently invisible in the moment it is being created.

It does not present as failure when it occurs. It presents as management. A project moves to next year's budget cycle because the current cycle is constrained. A maintenance contract is reduced in scope because the full scope is more than the current reserve allocation supports. An inspection interval is extended because the property appears to be in good condition and the saving can be applied elsewhere.

Each of these decisions, viewed in isolation, is defensible. The budget is constrained. The property appears fine. The savings are real. The board has acted reasonably within the information available to it.

Together, over time, they compound.

A surface crack in a parking structure becomes structural deterioration. A reduced maintenance scope for a waterproofing system becomes water intrusion that requires a remediation the original scope would have prevented. A delayed inspection misses the early-stage condition that, identified when it was small, would have cost $18,000 to address and, identified two years later, costs $95,000 to remediate.

I watched communities absorb this sequence for years before I understood that the sequence itself—not any individual decision within it—was the thing that needed to be made visible. Deferred maintenance does not reduce cost. It concentrates it. Every deferral is a transfer forward—a cost shifted into a future moment where it is unavoidable, urgent, and more expensive than it would have been if addressed when first identified.

The community that defers $30,000 in waterproofing maintenance for three years does not save $30,000. It converts $30,000 into $80,000 of emergency remediation, scheduled at a time that produces maximum disruption to residents, funded through an assessment that feels sudden because nobody tracked the sequence that produced it.

The CTI™ maintenance execution signal arrives before the reserve study confirms the deferred maintenance. That gap—between when homeowners begin describing maintenance as unresponsive and when the financial documents reflect the consequence—is the intervention window. The board that reads the signal can still change the trajectory. The board that waits for the reserve study is managing the aftermath.

PROCUREMENT OPACITY

The fourth risk operates through structure rather than timing, through relationship rather than neglect. It is the most difficult to surface through conventional means because it produces no visible failure. The community is maintained. The work is performed. The vendor shows up, completes the scope, and invoices the amount that was approved. From the outside, everything looks fine.

The problem is not the work. The problem is what the work cost relative to what it should have cost.

Chapter Seven described the incentive structure that produces procurement opacity. This chapter names the risk it creates for homeowners. That risk is not dramatic. It is persistent and compound.

A community that pays above-market rates for maintenance contracts year after year is not experiencing a crisis. It is experiencing a slow transfer of wealth—from the homeowners who fund the dues that pay the contracts, to the vendor ecosystem and management company relationships that capture the premium above market price.

What the homeowner cannot see is what comparable communities are paying for equivalent work. That comparative visibility—what the CTI™ maintenance execution dimension and market benchmark provide—is the instrument that makes procurement opacity visible for the first time.

The community whose CTI™ maintenance execution score is below the market benchmark while its maintenance spend is above comparable communities' averages is a community where procurement practices are producing cost without quality. That pattern is the signature of procurement opacity, expressed in the verified accounts of homeowners who are living with both the cost and the quality simultaneously.

THE CONSEQUENCES THAT EXTEND BEYOND THE HOMEOWNER

The four risks described in this chapter do not stay contained within the communities where they develop. They extend outward—into property values, into real estate transactions, into lending decisions, into the broader market for HOA-encumbered homes.

The homeowner who maintained her unit impeccably, who paid dues without a late payment, who participated in the community's governance as consistently as the system allowed, still absorbs the consequence of the community's condition at the moment of sale. The buyer evaluating a unit in a community with an underfunded reserve is evaluating a property whose long-term cost of ownership includes an assessment the current reserve study is already predicting. The lender underwriting a loan on that unit is underwriting collateral whose value is tied to a community whose financial trajectory is moving in a direction the loan's terms did not price.

The risks are collective. The consequences are individual.

The homeowner who bought in good faith, who did everything right at the unit level, inherits the governance decisions made at the community level by people whose terms may have ended before the consequence arrived.

This is the structural condition that makes invisible risk different from ordinary risk. Not that it exists—risks exist in every market. But that it is invisible at the moment when visibility would allow the person assuming it to make an informed decision about whether to assume it at all.

Visibility changes the sequence. Not by eliminating the risk. By moving the discovery earlier. Earlier discovery is the change that converts invisible risks into manageable ones.

The roof was fourteen years old. The reserve study had predicted the failure window. The contribution rate had not been adjusted to match it. The maintenance schedule had been built around budget constraints rather than condition monitoring.

None of the homeowners received a communication that translated the reserve study into a plain-language account of what was coming and when. None of them were shown the trajectory. They were given access to the document that described it and left to find it on their own.

The assessment was not a surprise to the system. It was a surprise to the people the system was supposed to serve.

That gap—between what the system knew and what the homeowner could use—is the gap the CTI™ is built to close.

Not after the assessment arrives.

Before.

CHAPTER 9

THE HOMEOWNER EXPERIENCE

The thing that was never built into the system

Sandra kept a folder.

It started with the first letter — a violation notice for a trash can visible from the street. She moved it within the hour. She kept the letter anyway.

By year seven she had eleven letters. Each documented a violation, a fine, a fee, or a demand. Not one had been preceded by a conversation, and not one had produced a response when she replied.

She showed me the folder at her kitchen table, set it down without saying anything, and waited.

That folder was not evidence of a bad HOA. It was evidence of a system with no obligation to behave any other way.

THE WRONG DIAGNOSIS

When an HOA relationship breaks down, the industry calls it a communication problem.

Better training. Better software. More homeowner involvement, more patience.

These explanations are not wrong — they are incomplete. They treat the outcome as the cause and assume a functional system populated by failing people.

Sandra's HOA was not an outlier. What she experienced was the default output of a system operating exactly as designed.

The design never included trust.

WHAT TRUST REQUIRES

Trust is not a feeling. It is a conclusion.

You trust an institution when consistent evidence confirms it will act in your interest — not occasionally, not when convenient, but reliably. That evidence has to come from somewhere.

In a functional institution it comes from transparency: visible financials, accessible records, rules applied consistently, an independent mechanism for the governed to verify what the governing claims.

The HOA system provides almost none of this by default.

Financials are disclosed on the board's schedule, minutes are produced when the board produces them, and enforcement is documented, reviewed, and appealed internally — with no independent auditor and no external standard.

Homeowners are asked to extend trust to an institution that provides almost no basis for it.

That is not a communication problem. That is an architecture problem.

THE EIGHT FRACTURE POINTS

Trust does not break all at once. It fractures across specific, repeatable contact points.

Governance. How decisions are made and whether homeowners have any real voice. In most communities: limited authority, board discretion, and no meaningful appeal.

Financial transparency. Where assessments go and how reserves are funded. The majority of HOAs in the United States operate with underfunded reserves, and most homeowners learn this only when the special assessment arrives.

Maintenance. Whether the physical community is kept as promised. Deferred maintenance is the most visible daily measure of board priorities.

Communication. Whether homeowners are informed before decisions are made, not after. Most HOA communication is reactive — it arrives when something has already gone wrong.

Enforcement. Whether rules apply equally. Selective enforcement destroys trust faster than any other failure. Nothing signals the power structure more clearly than watching a neighbor do what you were fined for.

Dispute resolution. What happens when a homeowner has a grievance. In most communities, the board investigates, reviews, and rules — with no independent mechanism and no external standard.

Participation. Whether the system is designed to include homeowners or process them. Most disengagement is not apathy. It is a rational calculation that engagement produces no outcome.

Emotional trust. The sum of all the above — the cumulative sense of whether this institution is fair, responsive, and on your side. Once gone, it does not return through a newsletter. It requires structural change.

THE CALCULATION HOMEOWNERS MAKE

After year three, Sandra stopped going to meetings.

She still paid her assessments and complied with every notice in the folder, but she stopped engaging in anything that required her to believe the system would respond.

The industry calls this apathy. It is not.

It is a rational response to eleven data points and zero evidence that participation produces results.

Why attend a meeting where the agenda is already decided? Why submit a request that will go unanswered? Why run for the board when the management company controls the procedures?

Disengagement is not the cause of the trust deficit. It is the proof of it.

When homeowners leave the room, the people who remain are the ones who benefit from low participation. The cycle does not self-correct. It deepens.

THE SCALE

Sandra's folder contains eleven letters. Multiply that by 75 million.

That is the number of Americans living in HOA-governed communities today — more than 30 percent of all U.S. housing, a share that has grown every decade since the 1960s.

The system governing that housing manages decisions about maintenance, finances, rules, and community character across an asset base exceeding $11 trillion in residential wealth.

A community with a broken trust relationship performs worse in the market. Buyers sense dysfunction before they can name it. Lenders flag underfunded reserves, underwriters price in governance risk, and realtors learn which communities to steer clients away from.

None of this is measured, standardized, or publicly accessible in any consistent form.

The trust deficit is not a soft problem. It is an $11 trillion data gap.

WHAT THE FOLDER MEANS NOW

Sandra still has the folder.

I asked her once if she would have bought the home if she had known. She thought about it.

She said she would have needed a score.

Not a perfect community, not a guarantee — just a number that told her, before she signed, that this institution had a verifiable track record and that other homeowners had documented their experience somewhere she could find it.

She did not want someone to fix the HOA. She wanted the information to make an informed decision.

That information did not exist when Sandra bought her home. For fifty years, tens of millions of homeowners have made one of the largest financial decisions of their lives with no trust data, no benchmark, and no score.

The folder on Sandra's kitchen table is not a record of a broken board.

It is a record of a broken standard.

And a broken standard is exactly the kind of problem that gets fixed — once someone decides to build the right instrument.

CHAPTER 10

WHY YOU STOPPED NOTICING

How dysfunction builds quietly – and why silence becomes rational

She had been on the email list for four years.

When she first moved in, she read every message — board updates, maintenance notices, annual meeting reminders. She attended the first meeting with questions on a notepad: the reserve fund, the landscaping contract, a pet policy she found genuinely ambiguous. She asked two of the three. One was answered. One was deferred to a subcommittee she was never told the outcome of.

The phrase "we'll take that offline" became the last thing she heard about it.

She attended the second annual meeting with fewer questions. The third with none. By the fourth year, emails arrived and were filed unread. HOA. Not urgent. Not worth the time, because processing them had not, in her experience, produced anything she needed to know.

She had not decided to stop paying attention. She had made a series of smaller decisions — each a marginal calculation about whether the next engagement would be worth the effort — and the sum was a homeowner who had opted out of governing the community she funded every month.

She did not think of herself as disengaged. She thought of herself as realistic.

She was right. That is the part the system rarely acknowledges.

A PATTERN ACROSS EVERY SYSTEM

What happened to her is not unique to housing. It is what every trust-dependent system produces when accountability becomes invisible and drift goes uncorrected.

People adjust their expectations to match what the system delivers rather than what it was designed to provide. Each adjustment is small. Collectively, they erase the standard. People lose sight of what good looks like — not because good disappeared, but because the distance between where the system started and where it now operates was covered in increments too small to trigger recognition.

What makes the HOA version distinctive is the combination of financial stakes, captive participation, and the near-total absence of external feedback. There is no competitor to reveal the gap. There is no opt-out that doesn't involve selling the home. And there is no independent signal that tells homeowners whether what they're experiencing is normal, exceptional, or a slow-moving failure.

That combination accelerates drift and removes the correctives other systems at least occasionally encounter.

THE PROBLEM WAS NEVER MOTIVATION

Low participation has long been treated as a behavioral problem. Boards ask why homeowners don't engage. The assumption is that more caring would produce more showing up.

Participation was never the issue. Design was.

In any system where feedback is optional, most people remain silent — not because they lack opinions, but because the system offers no visible return on engagement. No evidence that the effort produces a different outcome than the absence of effort.

A homeowner is not reviewing a product. She is evaluating the governance of her largest financial investment, and every input carries perceived risk: social risk, governance risk, and the risk that speaking up makes her visible to a system organized around enforcement. Without a benefit that clearly outweighs that risk, silence is the rational choice.

That is why participation has historically remained in the single digits. Not apathy. A correct response to the evidence the system provided.

HOW NOTICING STOPS

The first time a concern produces a genuine response, the homeowner learns that raising concerns works. The second time it produces an acknowledgment without resolution, she updates the probability. By the third or fourth data point, the calculation is complete.

She adjusts. Standards shift in increments no single interaction reveals. A three-day maintenance response becomes ten days, then two weeks, and nobody can point to the moment the standard changed — because there was no such moment. It eroded, one deferred response at a time, until the new norm became the expectation and the original standard became a memory no one could precisely locate.

This is calibration, not cynicism. She was not lowering her standards. She was aligning them to what the system actually delivered. The problem is not her calibration. The problem is a system that made accurate calibration require lowering expectations.

THE RISK THAT SPEAKING UP CARRIES

Calibration explains why homeowners stop expecting much. It does not explain why homeowners who notice significant problems still choose silence.

In communities organized around control rather than service, speaking up risks more than being ignored. The homeowner who raises a concern risks being noted — her identity logged, her future relationship with governance shaped by the fact of having raised something the system preferred not to address.

The violation notice that arrives two weeks after the board meeting where she asked the difficult question. The maintenance request that slows for the unit whose owner has been asking about procurement. The enforcement action that lands on the homeowner who organized her neighbors.

None of this can be proven retaliatory. That is its effectiveness. The pattern is visible to everyone and deniable by everyone responsible for it.

A fine takes minutes to levy and years to contest. The homeowner who has the time, the money, and the documentation can fight. Most calculate the cost and pay — not because they are wrong, but because being right is more expensive than surrendering.

That asymmetry is not incidental. It is the system working as designed.

THREE PATTERNS THAT SUSTAIN THE SILENCE

Disengagement is sustained by three patterns. Each is deniable in isolation. Together they form the architecture of a governance system organized around its own continuation.

Exhaustion. The homeowner who submits the same request three times and receives three acknowledgments without resolution stops submitting below a certain urgency. The system records the silence. It was an accurate reading of the system's response rate.

Removal through management. The homeowner who raises a concern and is talked past — subjected to the institutional condescension that signals her question reflects a misunderstanding — has been removed from participation without being made absent. The mechanism doesn't appear in the minutes. It lives in tone, in procedural complexity suddenly discovered when she asks to see a document, in the board president moving on before she finished.

Structural control. The nomination process technically open and practically managed. The committee promised and never formed. The agenda organized to consume available time before the item most likely to generate discussion reaches the floor. No one maintains these consciously. They persist through the inertia of institutions organized around stability rather than accountability.

She was not defeated. She was designed out — quietly, consistently, without a single moment she could point to.

WHAT SILENCE COSTS

The silence is not neutral. It is paid by the community as governance that drifts without correction.

The three-day maintenance response became two weeks because homeowners who once complained stopped complaining, and fourteen days became normal. The financial communication that stopped explaining the reserve trajectory stopped because asking produced the experience of being managed rather than informed.

Each adaptation removed the feedback the system needed to correct itself. That is the governance cost — not the toll on individual homeowners who gave up, but the removal of the signal that prevents quality from drifting toward whatever is most convenient for the parties producing it.

Multiply this across 350,000 HOA communities in the United States. The silence is not a collection of individual disappointments. It is the operating condition of a system that was never required to hear what it was producing.

WHAT THE SYSTEM RECORDED

She never submitted a complaint. She never missed a payment. She never violated a rule.

From the system's perspective, she was a satisfied homeowner.

The system had no mechanism to know otherwise. It was not designed to find out.

A governance system that cannot distinguish between satisfaction and surrender has no way to correct itself. It has no reason to try. It records silence as consensus and drift as stability — and it continues, undisturbed, until something from outside the system forces it to see what it has been producing.

CHAPTER 11

THE WINDOW OPENS

The moment clarity arrives – and what becomes possible once it does

He had owned the unit for nine years.

Nine years of dues, maintenance requests, meetings attended and skipped. Nine years inside a governance system he had stopped trying to understand around year four, when the effort stopped returning anything he could use.

One evening in October he opened a drawer looking for a certificate of insurance. He found it near the bottom. The drawer was already open. He kept looking.

He pulled out the three most recent reserve studies and laid them side by side.

The reserve fund had been at 74 percent funded six years ago. It was at 49 percent today. Contribution rates had increased twice — both times modestly, driven by pressure to keep dues stable rather than the trajectory the studies projected. Projected replacement costs had risen 31 percent from the first study to the third.

Every document had been properly sent, approved, disclosed. None of it had been hidden. What had been missing was the picture — the one no single document showed, and that nobody had assembled for him in nine years.

He was not angry. He was informed. For the first time in nine years, he understood the community he lived in.

WHAT THE DRIFT PRODUCES

Chapter 10 described how standards erode in increments no single interaction reveals. This chapter is about what happens when someone finally sees the distance.

The recalibration is automatic and invisible from inside it. Expectations adjust to match what exists rather than what was once possible. The reference point erodes alongside the standard until the adjusted expectation is the only one anyone can remember.

Then someone opens the drawer on a Tuesday evening. And the distance, which had been invisible for years, becomes measurable in thirty minutes.

That is what a window opening looks like. Not an event. A shift in position.

WHAT CLARITY CHANGES

Clarity does not change the past. The 74 to 49 percent decline is fixed. The contribution rate decisions that produced it are history.

What clarity changes is what you can do next.

He can now attend board meetings with specific questions — not general frustration, but the contribution rate required to close the gap before it becomes a special assessment. He can evaluate management company responsiveness against a standard he now understands. He can vote on dues increases knowing what the reserve fund actually requires rather than accepting the board's framing of what is reasonable.

Clarity does not create effort. It directs it. The homeowner without clarity has energy but no target. With clarity, the same energy finds the gaps the picture reveals — the gaps that have been producing consequences for years without anyone naming them.

THE MOMENT THE SYSTEM STOPS BEING INVISIBLE

There is a moment before any action — before the question, before the decision about what to do with what has just been seen.

It is the moment the system stops being background.

Not because it changed. Because the homeowner's position inside it did.

What you can see, you cannot unsee. He cannot experience the next dues increase as an arbitrary imposition. He knows what the reserve fund requires. He knows whether the proposed increase closes the gap or widens it. He is making an informed judgment about the governance of his community — possibly for the first time.

Informed judgments are the raw material governance depends on to function. For nine years, that material had been unavailable. Not withheld. Unassembled.

THE BUYER WHO SEES BEFORE SIGNING

The shift in an existing homeowner's position is consequential. The shift in a prospective buyer's position is transformative.

The homeowner who opened the drawer had nine years of context. The buyer thirty days into escrow has none. She is making a decision about a system she has never lived inside, in a window that does not allow for Tuesday evening assembly. She has the documents she has been given. She does not have a verified account of what living in this community is actually like, derived from the people who have been doing it.

The assembled picture — produced not by the institution being evaluated but by the verified homeowners who live inside it — provides what the documents cannot: a comparable, readable signal available in the time the transaction allows.

The buyer who sees a strong score makes a decision with eyes open. The buyer who sees a weak one — low marks on financial stewardship, maintenance execution, and community trust — sees the assembled picture before committing. She can negotiate differently, choose a different community, or proceed with full awareness of what she is entering.

Both decisions are valid. The difference is that now they are choices rather than guesses.

WHAT ACCOUNTABILITY ACTUALLY MEANS

Accountability in this context is not punishment. It is consequence.

The board whose governance quality is visible to every buyer now faces a market consequence for poor governance it did not previously have — not legal, not regulatory, but real. A declining score is a harder sell. A board member who wants to protect property values has a publicly visible signal telling them whether their decisions are contributing to that goal or working against it.

The management company whose performance is visible across its entire portfolio competes differently. Consistent above-benchmark results are a demonstrable advantage in a market that previously had no way to compare. Consistent below-benchmark results are a problem that preferred vendor relationships and long-term contracts cannot solve once the signal exists.

None of this requires a regulator. It requires a verified signal that makes performance visible — and a market that, once it can see performance, prices it accordingly. The signal is the mechanism. Visibility is the accountability.

WHAT THE WINDOW OPENING LOOKS LIKE

He submitted his first review three weeks after the October evening.

He described the 74 to 49 percent decline. The two modest contribution increases that hadn't matched projected need. The 31 percent rise in replacement costs the contribution rate had never been adjusted to reflect. The annual meetings where financial statements were presented without the context that would have made the trajectory visible.

He watched the score update. He could see his community against the market benchmark — comparable communities performing significantly better on financial stewardship and proactive communication.

He could see that he had been counted. For the first time, his experience existed outside of him. It was part of the permanent record of this community — visible to every person who would consider buying into it, living in it, or governing it.

He opened the next board meeting notification, registered to attend, and brought the three reserve studies.

The board was about to hear from a homeowner who had assembled the picture they had never assembled for him — with the market comparison showing exactly how far the community had drifted and exactly what closing that gap would require.

Not dramatic. Specific.

Specific is what changes things

PART II – THE STANDARD

The framework that makes the system visible—and measurable

CHAPTER 12

FROM EXPERIENCE TO STANDARD

In 1847, a Hungarian physician named Ignaz Semmelweis noticed something the hospitals around him had stopped noticing.

The maternity ward he worked in had a mortality rate that was three times higher than the ward next door. Women were dying of puerperal fever at a rate that anyone paying attention would have found alarming. Semmelweis paid attention. He tracked the difference between the two wards. He identified the variable. He implemented a protocol — physicians washing their hands with chlorinated lime solution before delivering babies — and the mortality rate in his ward dropped by ninety percent.

The medical establishment did not adopt his findings. They could not adopt them, because they had no framework for evaluating them. There was no standard against which Semmelweis's ward could be compared to every other ward. There was no measurement infrastructure that would have made the mortality gap visible to anyone who wasn't standing in his specific hallway watching it happen. His evidence was local. The problem was everywhere. And because there was no mechanism to convert local evidence into a standard the entire field could read, the gap between what Semmelweis knew and what medicine practiced remained open for another two decades, until Pasteur's germ theory finally provided the framework that made the evidence legible.

The cost of that gap was not abstract. It was paid by specific people, in specific wards, who died from a cause that one physician in Vienna had already identified and already solved.

This is what the absence of a standard costs. Not inefficiency. Not inconvenience. Preventable harm, sustained across time, because the evidence that could have corrected the problem existed only as local knowledge — held by people who had experienced it, invisible to the system that needed to act on it.

Every field that manages something that matters eventually builds a standard. Not because standards are philosophically appealing. Because the cost of not having one becomes visible enough that the field can no longer absorb it without consequence.

Aviation did not develop its safety protocols because pilots wanted more paperwork. It developed them because the alternative — a system in which each airline investigated its own accidents, drew its own conclusions, and implemented its own responses — was producing outcomes the industry could not sustain. The standard that emerged from that history was not a constraint on aviation. It was the infrastructure that made aviation the safest form of mass transportation in human history. What the standard did was convert local incident data — a crash here, a near-miss there, a mechanical failure in one aircraft type observed by one crew on one route — into a signal the entire industry could read, learn from, and build into the next generation of protocol.

Financial services built disclosure requirements not because the industry volunteered transparency but because the asymmetry between what institutions knew and what investors could find out had produced a specific category of harm often enough that the cost became politically impossible to ignore. The requirement did not eliminate the asymmetry. It narrowed it. It gave the person on the other side of the transaction a minimum level of information — standardized, comparable, independently verified — that made the decision they were about to make slightly less blind.

Medicine, aviation, finance. The pattern in each case was the same. An industry managing something with high stakes and significant quality variation. An extended period in which that variation was invisible because no standard existed to measure it. A cost, paid by specific people, that the field eventually could not defend. And then the standard — not as a reform imposed from outside, but as the correction of an absence that had become untenable.

The HOA system in 2025 is an industry managing something with high stakes and significant quality variation, in an extended period in which that variation is invisible, because no standard exists to measure it.

This is not a recent failure. It is the original condition of the industry. The HOA model that expanded across the American housing market in the second half of the twentieth century was not built with measurement in mind. It was built with administration in mind — a governance structure designed to manage shared property, enforce community rules, and collect the assessments that funded both. The question of how well it was doing these things, relative to other communities doing the same things, was never part of the architecture. There was no architecture for it. Each community governed itself, measured itself against its own history if it measured at all, and called the result governance.

What this produced, at scale, was a system with enormous variation in quality and no mechanism for making that variation visible. The community with a board that governed transparently, maintained reserves properly, communicated decisions clearly, and treated homeowners as the constituents they were — that community existed. So did its opposite. And the buyer moving from one to the other had no reliable way to know the difference before the purchase was complete and the consequences had begun.

The disclosure packet that the buyer receives before closing is not a solution to this problem. It is a document of record — governing documents, financial statements, meeting minutes — that tells the buyer what the association is required to disclose. What it does not tell them is what the homeowners who lived in that community would say if someone asked them whether those documents reflected the governance reality they actually experienced. The financial statement that shows a funded reserve does not show whether the board's decisions about how to fund it required three special assessments in the past decade. The meeting minutes that record a maintenance discussion do not show the pattern of response times that the homeowners who submitted requests over the past two years lived through.

The buyer is making one of the largest financial decisions of their life. They are receiving the minimum the law requires. The gap between those two things is the space in which the HOA system's accountability problem lives.

What converts individual experience into a standard is not volume. It is structure.

A thousand unstructured opinions about a community produce noise. A thousand verified homeowner reviews, structured across the same five dimensions, submitted through the same methodology, and aggregated into a score that can be compared to every other community in the dataset — that produces a standard. The difference between the two is not the number of voices. It is the architecture through which those voices are collected and the framework through which they are interpreted.

The CTI™ is that architecture.

The five dimensions — governance, financial stewardship, maintenance, communication, and emotional trust — are not categories chosen for convenience. They are the dimensions along which governed community life actually varies in ways that matter to the people living it. A community can be financially sound and governmentally opaque. It can maintain its physical infrastructure while failing to communicate what that maintenance costs or why. It can enforce its rules consistently in ways that produce resentment rather than safety. Each dimension captures something real about the governance environment that the others do not. Together, they produce a picture of the community that no single data point — not the reserve study, not the meeting minutes, not the management company's own performance report — has ever been able to produce.

The score that emerges from those five dimensions is not an opinion. It is a measurement. And a measurement, unlike an opinion, can be compared. It can establish a floor. It can identify a ceiling. It can tell a community not just how it is performing but how it is performing relative to every comparable community in the dataset — which is the only information that makes the score actionable.

This is what a standard does that a rating cannot. A rating tells you whether something was good or bad. A standard tells you where something sits in a distribution — and by doing so, tells every actor in the system what improvement looks like, what the gap is, and what closing that gap would require.

The board that receives a CTI™ report is receiving something no board in the history of HOA governance has ever received: a measurement of its performance against an external benchmark it did not produce and cannot dismiss. The management company whose portfolio appears in the dataset for the first time is seeing its performance across communities in a form that is independent of its own reporting. The buyer evaluating a community before making an offer is, for the first time, looking at a number that reflects the verified experience of the people who lived there — not the documents the association was required to produce.

None of these actors are being asked to trust the score. The score is built from verified homeowner experience, structured through a methodology that is independent of any party whose performance it measures, and comparable to a dataset that grows more meaningful as more communities join it. The standard does not require the industry's cooperation to be credible. It requires only that the people who have the experience be willing to record it — and that the architecture that receives that experience be rigorous enough to convert it into something the market can read.

What the market does with that signal is not a matter of persuasion. Every market that has acquired a reliable performance signal has incorporated it into decision-making, because the alternative — ignoring available information when making high-stakes decisions — is a discipline that markets do not sustain for long. Buyers will use the score because it tells them something they could not previously know. Lenders will incorporate it because it quantifies a risk they were previously absorbing without measuring. Management companies will compete on it because their clients will expect them to. Boards will respond to it because visibility without response is a governance posture that homeowners, buyers, and the market will no longer accept once the alternative is available.

Semmelweis had the answer in 1847. The field did not have the standard that would have made his answer legible until 1865, when Lister began applying germ theory to surgical practice and the evidence finally had a framework through which it could travel from one ward to every ward.

The homeowners who have been living inside poorly governed communities have had the experience for decades. They have known, specifically and personally, what the governance failure felt like and what it cost them. What they have not had is a mechanism to convert that experience into a signal the market could read — a standard that would make their local knowledge legible to every buyer, every lender, every board, every management company that needed to know where the floor was and what above it looked like.

The CTI™ is that mechanism. Not the first time anyone has tried to measure HOA performance. The first time anyone has built the architecture to convert verified homeowner experience, at scale, into a standard the market can price.

Experience goes in. Standard comes out. And the standard, once it exists, does what every standard in every field that has ever built one has done — it makes the cost of performing below it visible, and it makes ignoring that cost a choice that the market, over time, will not allow.

The absence of a standard is never neutral. It has a cost, and the cost is always paid by the person with the least information at the moment of the highest stakes decision. The HOA system has been collecting that cost from homeowners and buyers for fifty years. The CTI™ does not fix the system by reforming the people who run it. It fixes it by building the measurement layer that makes performance visible, comparison possible, and the cost of invisibility — for the first time — something the market can see.

CHAPTER 13

THE POWER OF REVIEWS

Why private experience produces private consequences–and what changes when experience becomes public

Her name was Margaret, and in the spring of 1987 she had a problem with her homeowners association that she could not resolve.

The problem was not dramatic. It was the kind that accumulates in managed communities when governance drifts and no one is watching from the outside. The enforcement had become inconsistent—the same rule applied to her unit that had not been applied to the unit three doors down, owned by someone she suspected had a closer relationship with the board. She had raised it. She had written a letter, specific and documented, describing the inconsistency with dates and photographs and the CC&R provision she believed applied to both situations equally. She had attended a board meeting and raised it in person. She had received, in response, the particular form of institutional non-acknowledgment that communicated clearly that her concern had been received and would not be acted upon.

She was frustrated. She was certain she was right. She had evidence.

She told her neighbor.

Her neighbor told two other neighbors. One of them had their own version of the same story—a different rule, the same inconsistency, the same experience of raising it and being managed rather than answered. The other had not had a problem with the board but found the account plausible and filed it away as information about the community she lived in.

The information traveled through the social network of the community the way information traveled in 1987: slowly, unevenly, through conversations that depended on who knew whom and who happened to be standing in the parking lot when the subject came up. It reached some homeowners. It did not reach others. It did not reach the homeowner who moved in six months later, who had no way of knowing the pattern existed, who would discover the same inconsistency herself eighteen months after moving in and go through the same sequence—letter, board meeting, non-acknowledgment—before making the same adjustment that Margaret had made.

Margaret moved out of the community four years later. The board member whose inconsistent enforcement had prompted her letter was still on the board. The pattern she had documented continued. The people who moved in after her had no way of knowing it existed—not because the information was hidden, but because the information was hers. Private. Contained inside her experience and the experiences of the neighbors she had managed to tell before she left.

The community absorbed her complaint. The system continued.

Nothing changed. Not because Margaret was wrong. Because her experience was private—and private experience produces private consequences.

THE SAME STORY, THIRTY YEARS FORWARD

Now move the same story forward thirty-seven years.

The same community. The same governance failure. The same homeowner, with the same documented evidence of inconsistent enforcement, the same unanswered letter, the same board meeting that produced nothing.

This time, she writes a review.

Three paragraphs. Specific. Calm. Organized around the dimensions that matter: the governance inconsistency she documented with dates and photographs, the communication she attempted and the response she received, the pattern she observed across multiple homeowners over eighteen months of living inside this governance system. Submitted through a platform that confirms she owns a unit in the community she is describing. Her ownership verified. Her identity protected. Her account permanent.

Published—not to her two neighbors in the parking lot, but to every buyer, realtor, lender, and board member who searches for this community's performance record from this moment forward.

The consequence is no longer contained within the social network of a single community. It is permanent. It is public. It is sitting on a page that the next buyer reads before making an offer—alongside the reviews of the seven other homeowners who had a version of the same experience and submitted their own accounts. The pattern that was invisible in 1987, scattered across private conversations that never aggregated into anything a decision-maker could see, is now a signal.

The board sees the governance dimension score. They see the AI-generated pattern summary across the open text comments. They see that comparable communities in the same market are scoring a full point higher on enforcement consistency.

Something changes.

Not because Margaret was more persuasive in 2024 than she was in 1987. Because in 2024, her experience was no longer private.

THE PROBLEM THAT REVIEWS SOLVE

Every system that eventually developed a review layer had the same underlying condition before it arrived: the people with the most accurate information about how the system performed were the people with the least ability to make that information useful.

The hotel guest who experienced a dirty room and an unresponsive front desk knew more about that hotel's actual performance than the travel agent booking it, the corporate account managing the relationship, or the hotel's own marketing materials. But the guest's knowledge was private. The hotel absorbed the complaint and continued.

The job candidate who survived a recruiting process that bore no resemblance to the actual working environment they entered knew more about that employer's culture than any job posting communicated. But their knowledge was private.

The homeowner who lived through a special assessment that the reserve study had been predicting for three years, who tried to engage with a governance system that responded only when it was ready to act on them—they knew more about that community's governance quality than any disclosure package communicated. But their knowledge was private.

In each case, the system's ability to continue performing poorly depended on the same structural condition: the people who knew the truth could not make it available to the people who needed it.

The review created that infrastructure. It made the customer's experience permanent, public, and organized in a form that the next customer can find before they decide. The HOA community that generated a special assessment the reserve study had been predicting now carries it forward as a CTI™ financial stewardship dimension below the market benchmark.

The system can no longer absorb the experience and move on. It must carry the experience forward. And systems that carry forward their failures adjust—not always quickly, but in the direction that the market signal points.

WHY THE CONSEQUENCE HAD TO BECOME PUBLIC

The review does not just inform the next decision. It changes the cost structure of the system being evaluated.

Before the review, the cost of a bad experience was contained. The hotel that delivered a poor experience absorbed the negative word-of-mouth from guests who mentioned it to friends and continued. The HOA that generated a special assessment sent out the notices and continued. The cost of the failure stayed inside the institution, small enough to absorb, infrequent enough to manage.

After the review, the cost is permanent and cumulative. The hotel that accumulates three-star reviews in a four-star market loses bookings. The HOA community that accumulates low CTI™ scores loses buyers—or loses them to a lower offer price that reflects the risk discount the market applies to communities it cannot trust.

This is what changes behavior. Not awareness. Not intention. Consequence. The real, measurable, market-priced consequence of performance that is now visible in a form the market can read and act on.

The system that once absorbed failure must now carry it forward. And systems that carry forward failure adjust their behavior to produce less of it. Not because they developed better values. Because the cost of producing failure changed.

THE PATTERN ACROSS INDUSTRIES

Every major service system that influences outcomes at scale eventually develops a review layer. The mechanism varies. The resistance from institutions being evaluated varies. The outcome does not.

Hospitality developed it first and most completely. The transformation following TripAdvisor and the major booking platforms is the most documented case study in how public performance visibility reshapes service delivery at scale. Hotels that had operated for decades with internal quality metrics as their primary performance signal suddenly had an external, public, unfiltered account of what guests actually experienced. Pricing, occupancy, and reputation became directly tied to the visible record.

Employment developed its version more recently through Glassdoor—and the pattern repeated. Employers who had operated without external accountability for their workplace culture suddenly had a public record of what employees experienced. Recruiting, retention, and employer brand all moved in response.

Financial services developed its version through regulatory requirement rather than market mechanism—the CFPB complaint database, state licensing requirements, public enforcement records.

The HOA system was the exception. Fifty-five million homes. Eleven trillion dollars in residential wealth. One hundred forty billion dollars in annual dues. An industry that touches more Americans' daily financial lives than almost any other—and until recently, no public, verified, standardized account of what it was actually like to live inside it.

That exception is ending. The question is not whether the review layer will produce in the HOA market what it produced in every other. The question is how quickly.

WHAT MAKES A REVIEW SYSTEM WORK

Not every review system produces the accountability its designers intended. The history of online reviews is also a history of manipulation, gaming, and the gradual erosion of credibility that follows when verification is insufficient.

Four structural requirements determine whether a review system produces signal or noise. The CTI™ is designed around all four.

The first is verification. The review that anyone can submit, regardless of whether they have any connection to what they are reviewing, is a review that any motivated party can game. The CTI™ verification requirement—ownership of a unit in the community being reviewed, confirmed through a process the reviewer did not design and cannot manipulate—removes the gaming vector that has corrupted most consumer review systems. The score reflects only the people who actually live there.

The second is structure. The unstructured review that asks only for a star rating and a comment produces information that cannot be compared. The CTI™ five-dimension framework ensures every review addresses the same dimensions in the same terms—so that a community's maintenance execution score means the same thing this quarter as it did last quarter, and the same thing as the score of the community two miles away.

The third is permanence. The review that disappears after six months, or that the institution being reviewed can request removed, is a review the institution can outlast rather than respond to. The CTI™ record is permanent. It can only be improved—by changing the governance practices that produced it.

The fourth is scale. A review system with twelve participants in a market of ten thousand is a curiosity, not a standard. The CTI™ becomes a standard when enough communities participate that the benchmark is empirical rather than theoretical. Each new community that joins makes every existing community's score more meaningful. Each new homeowner who participates makes the signal more representative.

Verification removes manipulation. Structure creates comparability. Permanence creates accountability. Scale creates standards. Together, they produce a signal that cannot be gamed, cannot be ignored, and cannot be reversed once it has been built.

THE THRESHOLD THE HOA SYSTEM IS CROSSING

Every market standard crosses a threshold—a point at which the standard shifts from something some participants have adopted to something the market expects every participant to have. Before the threshold, the absence of the standard is unremarkable. After it, the absence is a statement.

The HOA system is crossing that threshold now.

In the markets where CTI™ participation has reached critical mass—where enough communities have been building verified homeowner records long enough that buyers, realtors, and lenders have begun incorporating the signal into their standard processes—the community without a score is no longer unparticipating. It is making a choice. And in a market that has learned to read the choice, the community that chooses invisibility is telling the market something about what visibility would reveal.

That threshold is not a single moment. It is a progression. The arc does not reverse. Standards do not un-become standards. The walkability score did not disappear from MLS listings when some neighborhoods scored poorly. It became the mechanism by which neighborhoods that scored poorly were held accountable to the buyers who could now see the score.

The CTI™ arc ends in the same place. Not because anyone required it. Because the market that could see performance began to expect it—and expectations, once formed at scale, reshape the behavior of every participant in the system.

The experience that was private is becoming public.

And public experience changes behavior.

That is the threshold. And once crossed, it does not reverse.

MARGARET'S REVIEW

She would be in her seventies now, if she is still alive. The community she left in 1991 has changed several times since—new management companies, new board compositions, new homeowners who moved in without knowing any of the history that she carried out with her when she left.

The structural condition that made her experience private—that made the information she held impossible to share with the people who needed it at the moment they needed it—that condition persisted for thirty-seven years after she left. The homeowners who came after her went through versions of the same sequence. Some of them told their neighbors. Some of them wrote letters that were received and filed.

None of them had a mechanism that made their experience consequential beyond the walls of the community they lived in.

That mechanism exists now.

The homeowner who is living through what Margaret lived through in 1987—who has the documented evidence, who has written the letter, who has attended the board meeting and been managed rather than answered—has something Margaret did not have.

She has a platform that confirms she lives where she says she lives. That protects her identity while establishing her standing. That publishes her verified account permanently, on a public page, in a form that every future buyer will read before deciding whether to make an offer.

She has eleven minutes and a mechanism that makes those eleven minutes matter beyond the conversation in the parking lot.

The experience that was private is now public.

The consequence that was contained is now permanent.

And the system that absorbed Margaret's complaint and continued is the system that, encounter by encounter, review by review, community by community, is becoming a system that cannot.

AUTHORITY DRIFT™

Why behavior changes in HOA meetings–and how reviews restore balance

Across many communities, I began to notice the same pattern. Different buildings. Different boards. Different personalities. The details changed. The pattern did not.

A homeowner would raise a question—often reasonable, often supported with facts. The response would come quickly. Sometimes technically correct. Sometimes final in tone. The moment would pass. The meeting would move on. Nothing inappropriate had occurred in a way that would be recorded or remembered as an incident. But something had changed.

The next time, that same homeowner would ask a shorter question. The phrasing would soften. The confidence would narrow. Or the question would not be asked at all. Over time, more people did the same. Meetings became quieter. Fewer hands went up. Discussions shortened. Decisions moved forward with less visible resistance.

From the Board's perspective, this could look like progress. Fewer interruptions. More efficient meetings. A sense that alignment had been achieved. But the quiet was not coming from agreement. It was coming from caution.

What was being observed was not resolution. It was adaptation.

STRUCTURE SHAPES BEHAVIOR

This pattern is not unique to HOAs. It has been studied before, in different contexts, under different conditions. In 1971, psychologist Philip Zimbardo conducted what became known as the **Stanford Prison Experiment**. The study placed ordinary individuals into a structured environment where some were assigned positions of authority and others were placed in subordinate roles. No one was instructed to behave harshly. No one was selected for a particular personality profile. The structure alone did the work.

Within a short period of time, behavior shifted. Those in positions of authority became more directive, more certain, and more controlling in how they interacted with others. Those without authority became quieter, more cautious, and more likely to comply rather than challenge. The study has been debated and criticized over the years, and it should not be taken as a perfect model of real-world systems. Its central insight, however, remains influential: when authority is clear, feedback is limited, and roles are reinforced without continuous correction, behavior changes.

The lesson is not about prisons. It is about structure.

HOA communities are not comparable in purpose or severity, but the structural elements are familiar enough to produce similar patterns over time.

STRUCTURAL PARALLEL

Assigned authority ("guards") → Board President / Board
Subordinate role ("prisoners") → Homeowners
Rules enforced without debate → CC&Rs and enforcement actions
Limited oversight of authority → Minimal real-time accountability
Behavior becomes more controlling → Tone becomes sharper, more final
Others withdraw or comply → Homeowners speak less or not at all

The comparison is not literal. The behavior pattern is.

When authority is concentrated and feedback is unstructured, two things begin to happen at the same time. Leadership becomes more confident and more directive in how it communicates. Homeowners become more selective and more cautious in how they respond. Neither side intends this outcome. Both sides adjust to the conditions they are operating within.

What homeowners feel in these moments is rarely stated directly. It shows up in small calculations that happen in real time. The question forms, but it is edited before it is spoken. The comment is reframed to reduce the chance of pushback. The decision is made, quietly, that this is not the setting to raise a concern that may not be received well.

Silence, in this context, is easy to misinterpret. It can look like agreement. It can look like satisfaction. It can look like a well-run meeting moving efficiently toward decisions. But in many communities, silence means something else.

Silence in an HOA is not agreement. It's information that never made it into the system.

When that shift occurs, the system begins to lose something essential. Governance, in its simplest form, is not just the act of making decisions. It is the ability of a system to receive, process, and respond to input from the people it represents. When that input narrows—not because the issues have disappeared, but because the conditions for expressing them have changed—the system does not become more effective. It becomes less informed.

I heard this dynamic expressed directly in a conversation with a board member from a large association. He said, without hesitation, "Only the complainers will review." He followed it with a second observation: "**Our board is very tight**. We don't want to be criticized." Neither statement was delivered with hostility. Both were presented as practical realities.

Taken at face value, they are understandable. Boards are composed of volunteers. They manage real responsibilities with limited time. The concern that feedback may be skewed toward negative experiences feels reasonable. The desire to maintain cohesion within the board feels necessary. But these beliefs, when acted upon, produce a predictable outcome.

They reduce visible feedback.

And when visible feedback is reduced, it is not eliminated. It is displaced.

The homeowner who chooses not to speak in a meeting does not lose their experience. They relocate it. It moves into private conversations, small groups, and informal networks where information is shared without structure, without verification, and without the ability to be aggregated into something a decision-maker can use. The system continues to operate, but it operates with less information than the people inside it actually have.

From the Board's point of view, the environment may feel stable. From the homeowner's point of view, it may feel constrained. The gap between those two perceptions is where problems begin to grow. It is also where reputation begins to form, quietly, long before it becomes visible.

DEFINING AUTHORITY DRIFT

This is the pattern I refer to as Authority Drift.

Not as a judgment of individuals. Not as a claim that any particular Board is acting with intent to control. It is a description of what happens when leadership operates without a clear, continuous view of how it is being experienced. Authority Drift begins subtly. It is not a single moment or a specific decision. It is the gradual shift in tone, responsiveness, and participation that occurs when feedback becomes limited and visibility declines.

Over time, the effects become measurable. Participation narrows. Communication feels more final. Homeowners adjust their behavior. Trust, which is built through repeated interactions over time, begins to weaken in ways that are not immediately visible but are consistently felt.

Most Board Presidents do not see this as it is happening. From inside the role, the experience is different. The focus is on moving meetings forward, managing agendas, making decisions, and addressing issues that require attention. The signals that would indicate a change in how those actions are being received are not readily available. Without a structured way to see them, they are easy to miss.

HOW REVIEWS RESTORE BALANCE

This is where reviews change the system.

Reviews do not create new problems. They make existing patterns visible. They take information that would otherwise remain private and place it into a structure that can be seen, measured, and understood. When homeowners are able to share their experience in a way that is verified but protected—where their connection to the community is confirmed, but their identity is not exposed—the cost of participation changes.

The individual no longer has to stand alone to be heard.

The information can enter the system without becoming a personal confrontation. It can be combined with other experiences, compared across time, and understood as part of a pattern rather than as an isolated complaint. This is the difference between a single voice and a measurable signal.

A system doesn't improve by avoiding bad information. It improves by seeing all of it–good, bad, or ugly.

When that signal appears, it does not function as criticism in the way it is often assumed. It functions as visibility. Boards can see how communication is being received. They can see where homeowners feel heard and where they do not. They can see how their community compares to others operating under similar conditions. The information that was previously unavailable becomes accessible in a form that can be acted on.

At that point, Authority Drift is no longer hidden. It becomes something that can be recognized and addressed.

This is not about changing personalities. It is about restoring the feedback loop that governance depends on to function effectively. When Boards can see how they are being experienced, they can make adjustments. They can create space for questions to be fully heard. They can explain decisions in ways that reduce uncertainty. They can signal, through consistent behavior, that participation does not carry the cost it once did.

ROLES AND RESPONSIBILITIES

Property management companies play a critical role in this process. They operate across multiple communities. They see patterns that individual Boards cannot see on their own. When Authority Drift appears in review data—through lower communication scores, repeated language that indicates homeowners feel dismissed, or declining participation signals—it should be treated as an early indicator of a system that is beginning to lose alignment.

The responsibility at that point is not to defend the Board. It is to help the Board see what is happening while it is still early enough to adjust. This requires clarity and neutrality. It requires treating feedback as performance data rather than as opposition.

Boards, in turn, have a role that is equally important. They should understand that this pattern exists, that it is common, and that it is not a reflection of failure in intent. It is a reflection of how systems behave when feedback is limited. Recognizing Authority Drift does not require agreement with every piece of feedback. It requires an understanding that the pattern itself carries information that is useful.

Boards that understand this early outperform those that don't.

When that happens, the outcomes begin to change. Communication becomes clearer. Participation increases. Decisions are better understood. Trust, which cannot be mandated but can be built through consistent experience, begins to strengthen.

STRUCTURE AND FEEDBACK

The Stanford experiment demonstrated that structure shapes behavior. HOA communities operate within structures that can either limit or enable feedback. When feedback is limited, behavior drifts. When feedback is visible, behavior adjusts.

Reviews don't just measure performance. They restore the visibility that makes trust possible.

Authority Drift is not the product of bad intentions – it is the predictable result of governance operating without visible feedback. Reviews restore the signal that makes correction possible.

STATUS OCCUPANCY

When presence replaces participation–and how visibility restores standards

There is another pattern that appears across many communities. It does not present with tension or conflict, and it rarely draws attention in a single moment. It presents quietly, through conditions that change slowly enough to be accepted before they are questioned.

Board members are present. Meetings occur. Decisions are made. On paper, the system is functioning as expected. But when you look at the community itself—what is actually happening on the ground—a different picture begins to form. Streetlights burn out and remain that way longer than they should. Landscaped areas begin to fade and are not restored to their prior condition. Trees die and stand for extended periods before action is taken.

These are not hidden problems. They are visible to anyone who lives in the community. Residents pass them every day. They notice them without effort, and over time, they begin to adjust their expectations around them. What was once an exception becomes something that is simply part of the environment.

The gap that forms in these situations is not a gap in authority. It is a gap in attention.

THE GAP IN ATTENTION

The board's responsibility is directly tied to the condition of the community, yet the level of observation required to maintain that condition is not always consistently applied. Meetings are attended. Agendas are followed. Decisions are approved. The system moves forward. But governance is not measured by motion. It is measured by condition. When conditions are not actively observed, they do not improve. What isn't inspected does not improve.

In some cases, the role itself becomes sufficient. The title carries meaning. It signals involvement and establishes a position within the structure of the community. Over time, that can create a sense that the responsibility is being fulfilled simply by participating in the formal aspects of governance. Not because the individual intends to disengage, but because the system continues to function without requiring deeper engagement.

Nothing breaks all at once in this environment. A light goes out and is noted but not followed. An area becomes unmaintained and is seen, but not prioritized. A tree dies and remains in place longer than it should. Each instance is small, and each can be explained in isolation. Taken together, however, they form a pattern. The standard begins to move—not sharply, but steadily downward.

Like Authority Drift, the consequences are delayed. There is no immediate signal that something is wrong. The system continues to operate, and on the surface, it appears stable. Over time, however, the appearance of the community changes. The sense of care begins to weaken, and small issues that would have been addressed early begin to accumulate into larger ones. The system is no longer improving. It is maintaining a lower standard.

Residents do not track this formally, but they experience it consistently. They notice which lights remain out, which areas are not maintained, and how long it takes for issues to be addressed. They may not raise these observations in meetings, but they carry the information with them. Over time, that information shapes how they view the community they live in.

HOW REVIEWS CHANGE THE SYSTEM

This is where the introduction of reviews begins to change the system.

When homeowners begin to describe what they are seeing—consistently, across multiple reviews—the information that was previously scattered becomes organized. Lighting is mentioned in more than one account. Maintenance appears in similar terms across different homeowners. Responsiveness is described in ways that begin to align. What had been isolated observations becomes a visible pattern.

Once that pattern is visible, the response begins to change.

Boards and management companies start to observe the community differently. They drive the property at night and see lighting conditions across the entire environment rather than in isolated areas. They walk the grounds with a clearer understanding of what is maintained and what is not. They review logs not as a record of activity, but as something that must align with what residents are actually experiencing.

The work becomes more intentional. Scope-of-work documents are clarified. Standards are defined in a way that can be measured. Vendor performance is evaluated against conditions that are visible rather than assumed. The shift is not driven by pressure. It is driven by clarity.

When expectations become visible, execution follows.

The board understands what requires attention. The management company aligns to those expectations. Vendors respond to standards that are now defined and observed. The system becomes connected again.

As conditions improve, something else becomes visible. Homeowners begin to notice the difference. Lighting becomes consistent. Maintenance becomes reliable. Issues are addressed in a way that can be seen. This appears in the review system not as isolated praise, but as a pattern of satisfaction. That pattern reinforces the standard in the same way that earlier patterns revealed its decline.

ROLES AND ACCOUNTABILITY

For boards, the lesson is direct. Holding a position is not the same as performing it. The role requires attention to what is actually happening within the community. It requires seeing conditions directly, asking questions about what is being reported, and following through on what is observed. When that level of engagement is present, the system improves in ways that are visible to everyone who lives there.

For management companies, the signal is equally clear. When engagement is low, decisions tend to be accepted without depth, conditions are not fully observed, and performance becomes inconsistent over time. This is not a stable condition. It is one that requires active correction. Strong management teams respond by bringing visibility to conditions, aligning boards with clear standards, and ensuring that execution matches what is expected.

This pattern is not about control. It is about the absence of engagement. It is what I refer to as Status Occupancy — a condition where the role is filled, but the function is only partially performed. A title can hold authority. Only engagement creates governance.

Standards do not rise on intention. They rise on what is seen, measured, and repeated.

Reviews do not introduce new problems. They reveal what has been overlooked. And once something is visible, it can be acted on. That is where standards begin to rise, where performance becomes consistent, and where trust is built.

Status Occupancy is not dereliction — it is the quiet drift that occurs when a title substitutes for attention. Reviews restore the visibility that turns presence back into participation.

CHAPTER 14

THE COMMUNITY TRUST INDEX™

What the standard measures, how it works, and why it matters

She had been looking for a home for four months.

The market was hard. Good homes sold fast. She lost her first offer to someone who bid more. She pulled out of her second after an inspection found water damage the seller would not fix. She made a third offer on a home she was not sure about and felt relieved when she did not get it.

The fourth felt right from the first visit. The home was right. The area was right. The price, after two rounds of back and forth, was right. The inspection came back clean. The bank had approved her loan. It felt like a done deal.

She was thirty-one days from closing when the appraiser called.

The appraiser had been doing this job for nineteen years. She could walk into a building and sense when things were being ignored. She could read a financial report fast enough to know if the numbers matched what she was seeing. She knew that two homes that looked the same could carry very different risk — and that the difference was rarely in the unit itself.

The reserve study was three years old. The monthly contribution rate was below what the study said it should be. The management company had changed eighteen months earlier, and that transition had left gaps in the financial records she could see but not fully explain.

She told the buyer what she had found. The buyer listened. Then she asked the question that nineteen years of professional experience could not answer.

"Is it a good community to live in?"

The appraiser paused.

She did not know. Not because she lacked skill. Because the tool needed to answer that question honestly — a verified, comparable score built from what people actually experienced living there — did not exist.

The buyer closed anyway. She had run out of time, and the home was right in every way she could measure.

Fourteen months later, a bill arrived. A special assessment. The HOA needed money fast. The reserve study had been predicting it for three years.

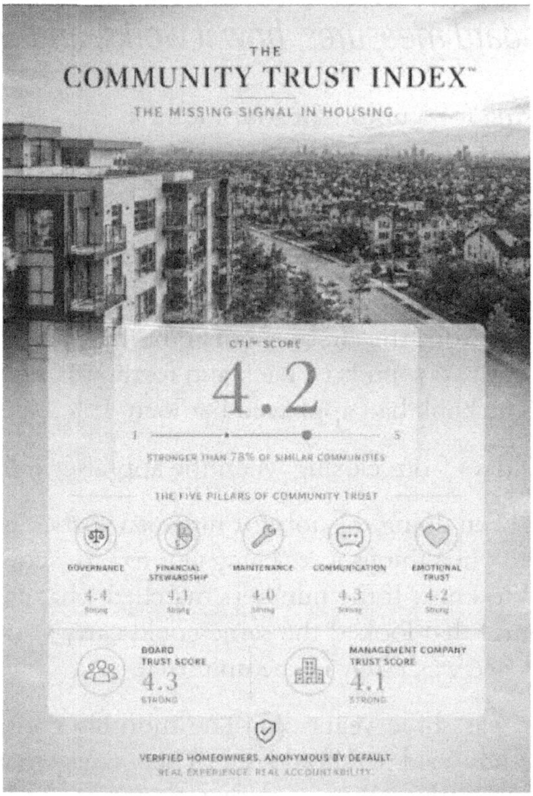

THE PROBLEM WITH HOW HOAS ARE MEASURED

Most attempts to evaluate HOA performance have failed for the same reason: the wrong parties are doing the measuring.

The HOA writes its own financial reports. The management company writes its own performance summaries. Industry groups certify the very companies that pay to join them. Every one of these sources has a structural interest in the result — so every one of them, without lying, tends to produce findings that reflect well on the party producing them.

The homeowner has no such interest. When a verified homeowner describes what it is like to live in their community, they want the truth — because the truth protects their home and their investment. A report that makes the management company look better than it is protects the management company's contract. An honest report protects the homeowner's equity.

That is where the Community Trust Index™ begins. Not with a scoring methodology, but with a foundational rule about who should be doing the talking.

The CTI™ is built on what verified homeowners say. Not what the board says about how the community is being run. Not what the management company says about how it is being managed. What the people who actually live there say it is like. That rule changes what the score can be used for, who can produce it, and why no institution being measured can manufacture the result.

TWO SCORES, ONE NUMBER, EQUAL WEIGHT

The CTI™ score — shown on a scale of one to five — is the average of two separate scores: the Board Trust Score and the Management Company Trust Score.

That separation reflects the most consequential distinction in HOA governance. The board sets policy. The management company executes it. These are different jobs with different responsibilities and different failure modes. Combining them into a single undifferentiated number conceals the problem precisely when clarity is most needed.

When a repair request goes unanswered for six weeks, is that a board failure or a management company failure? When financial reports arrive late and unintelligible, who is responsible — the board or the company it hired? When rules are enforced against some homeowners and overlooked for others, is that a policy problem or an execution problem? A blended score cannot answer these questions. The CTI™ answers them by keeping the scores separate, then combining them equally into the final number.

Equal weight is the most important design decision in the system. A board that governs well but contracts a management company that performs poorly will see that underperformance in the final score. A management company that executes well but serves a board that governs badly will carry those governance failures in the score too. Neither side can be fixed in isolation. The score will reflect it either way.

THE FIVE PILLARS

The CTI™ measures five areas of community life. Each is scored separately for the board and for the management company — twenty-two questions in total, eleven directed at the board and eleven at the management company, producing ten individual scores that combine into two trust scores and then into the final number.

PILLAR ONE: GOVERNANCE

Governance measures fairness. Are rules applied consistently across all homeowners? Are decisions made transparently? Is the homeowner treated as a person the community serves or a problem the community manages?

The board questions examine whether rules are clear, applied without favoritism, and made through visible processes. The management company questions examine whether those rules are actually carried out that way day to day. A board can establish fair policy and still have a management company that applies it unevenly. A management company can execute faithfully and still produce unfair outcomes if the policy itself is not equitable. When the board score and management company score in this pillar diverge sharply, the source of the problem — and the location of the fix — becomes specific rather than general.

PILLAR TWO: FINANCIAL STEWARDSHIP

Financial stewardship measures how money is planned and reported. Is the board building reserves adequate to meet predictable future costs? Is the management company presenting finances in a format homeowners can actually read and act on?

The board questions focus on long-term planning — whether the HOA is funding reserves at a rate that keeps large expenses from arriving as emergencies. The management company questions focus on clarity — whether the reports homeowners receive reflect what is actually happening with their money. A community can maintain sound finances and still report them in a way that produces confusion rather than confidence. The CTI™ scores both dimensions separately, because homeowners need both to trust the system managing their investment.

PILLAR THREE: MAINTENANCE

Maintenance is the pillar homeowners experience most directly. Is the physical property being maintained, or deferred? Are problems identified and addressed before they compound? Are vendors performing to standard?

The board questions focus on oversight — whether the board selects capable vendors, manages contracts with rigor, and treats maintenance as a strategy for protecting long-term asset value rather than a cost to delay. The management company questions focus on execution — whether the work that was authorized is actually being done well and on schedule.

The financial stakes of this pillar are concrete. A roof coating completed on schedule costs a fraction of a full roof replacement. An elevator component replaced during planned maintenance costs far less than an emergency failure. The gap between those two numbers is a decision the board makes — often years before the bill arrives. Maintenance scores expose that decision early. When homeowners consistently rate maintenance poorly, the physical deterioration that produces special assessments is already accumulating, often before it appears in any financial report.

PILLAR FOUR: COMMUNICATION

Communication measures whether the homeowner is treated as someone to inform or someone to manage. Does the community share information before decisions are made, or only after consequences have arrived? Are the reasons behind decisions explained, or only the outcomes announced?

The difference is immediate and felt. A homeowner who receives a fine without prior notice has been managed. A homeowner who receives a clear explanation of what the reserve fund is doing and why assessments are changing has been served. Before the consequence, not after — that is what proactive means. Showing the reason, not just the result — that is what transparent means. The board questions ask whether the board meets both standards. The management company questions ask whether it makes that standard of communication operationally possible.

PILLAR FIVE: EMOTIONAL TRUST

The first four pillars measure what a community does. Emotional Trust measures whether homeowners believe the community is doing it for them.

This pillar captures something harder to quantify: whether the board and management company are actually oriented toward the people they serve. Not through a direct question about intentions — intentions cannot be scored — but through the accumulated weight of daily interactions. Was a question welcomed or shut down? Was a concern logged or genuinely addressed? Was a request handled or deflected into procedure?

Emotional Trust uses two inputs. The first is a standard 1–5 rating that feeds directly into the score alongside the other four pillars. The second is the Community Voice question: an open-text field where homeowners describe in their own words what the community does well and what it should improve. These written responses do not enter the score. Instead, they are analyzed across all verified submissions for that community and cycle, surfacing repeated language, shared concerns, and consistent patterns. The result appears in the board and management company dashboard each quarter: a plain-language summary of what verified homeowners are consistently saying, with no institution in between.

A board can work to raise a number. No board can control what happens when dozens of verified homeowners, writing independently and protected by anonymity, describe the same experience in the same words. That is what makes Emotional Trust the hardest pillar to manipulate — not because the question is difficult to answer honestly, but because the written record beneath it cannot be staged.

THE VERIFICATION THAT MAKES IT REAL

The CTI™ score means something for one reason: it can only be produced by verified homeowners. Not review farms. Not management companies submitting assessments of their own properties. Not boards improving their own scores. Only confirmed owners — people whose name is on the deed of a unit in that community — describing what it is actually like to live there.

The HOA market runs on self-reported data. Financial summaries written by the institutions they describe. Performance reports produced by the companies being evaluated. Certification programs administered by the same industry organizations that sell memberships to the companies being certified. What the market has almost never had is a score the institution being measured cannot produce on its own behalf. Verification is what makes the CTI™ categorically different from everything that preceded it.

The verification process confirms ownership without revealing identity. The homeowner knows their ownership has been established and their name is protected. Both facts together are what make honest participation possible at scale — and what make the resulting score credible to everyone who uses it.

ANONYMOUS BY DEFAULT

Every homeowner who submits a CTI™ review is anonymous by default. Ownership is confirmed. Identity is not attached to the score.

This is not a privacy feature. In communities where leadership has abused its authority, it is the condition that makes honest participation possible at all. Homeowners who have spoken up about governance problems have faced documented retaliation — fines, selective enforcement, social pressure, neighbor-against-neighbor dynamics deployed by boards with no outside check on their behavior. These are not hypothetical risks. They are the predictable outcome of a system that operated without accountability for decades.

Anonymous by default removes the calculation entirely. The homeowner does not weigh whether telling the truth is worth the consequence. They submit knowing their ownership is confirmed and their name is protected — and they tell the truth. That truth, collected from every verified homeowner who participates, is the signal the market has been missing.

TWICE A YEAR

The CTI™ runs twice a year — spring and fall. Eleven minutes each cycle. This is not a one-time assessment. It is a recurring record.

The cadence matters for two reasons. First, communities change. Boards turn over. Management companies get replaced. A community that scored well eighteen months ago may have since gone through a contested election, a management transition, and a major construction dispute. A single historical score does not reflect where the community is now. Second, two data points per year reveal direction. One score is a position. Two scores per year show movement — whether things are improving, holding, or declining. A community whose spring score is stable and whose fall score drops is telling a story neither score tells in isolation.

Twice a year. Eleven minutes. That is the cost of a continuous, verified record of how a community is actually performing — produced by the only people in the system with no institutional reason to misrepresent the answer.

THE SIGNAL THAT WAS ALWAYS MISSING

The buyer who closed anyway was not being reckless. She made the best decision available to her with the information she had. The information she had was not enough.

Fourteen months later she was managing a special assessment the reserve study had been predicting for three years. The appraiser had sensed something was wrong. The documents had contained the warning. Nineteen years of professional experience had pointed toward it. None of it produced the one thing that would have changed the outcome.

A clear, verified score — before she signed — reflecting what it was actually like to live in that community.

That score exists now. A set of questions, asked of verified homeowners, across five areas that together capture how a community is governed and managed. Scored separately for the board and management company. Weighted equally so neither side can improve its standing by pointing to the other. Combined into a single number anyone can find before the decision is made.

Once a standard exists — once a buyer can see the community before she commits to it, once a board can measure itself against comparable communities in its market, once a management company's record is visible in a benchmark it did not create and cannot alter, once the homeowner who was silenced at a meeting has a permanent and protected place to put the truth she was not permitted to speak out loud, once the agent advising a client can finally answer the question that nineteen years of experience could not — the system that operated without one for fifty years has to answer something it has never been asked.

How does your community measure up?

The signal was always there. It was the structure to collect it, verify it, and make it visible that was missing. That structure exists now.

CHAPTER 15

THE LEAST YOU CAN DO (START HERE)

Why the barrier was never the problem – and what changes when the return finally matches the effort

She had tried everything the system offered.

She had attended board meetings — three in two years, which was three more than most of her neighbors. She had submitted maintenance requests through the portal the management company provided, tracking each one through the automated acknowledgment that arrived within minutes and the silence that followed for weeks. She had sent emails, left voicemails, and spoken during the public comment period about the enforcement pattern she had documented — specific, calm, supported by dates and unit numbers — and received, in response, an acknowledgment that the matter would be reviewed, followed by no review she could detect.

She tried. The system had absorbed her effort and continued.

She was not unusual in this. She was the standard homeowner engagement story: someone who cared enough to participate, used every mechanism available, and received a return so consistently disproportionate to the effort that she made the rational decision to stop. Not because she stopped caring, but because she stopped expecting that caring would produce a result.

This is the cycle the earlier chapters described: comfort, friction, confusion, resignation. She reached that final stage not through indifference, but through experience. The system had taught her, through repetition, that engagement did not produce outcomes proportional to the cost of engaging.

Now the platform exists. Now her community can join. Now she can submit a verified homeowner review that does what her letters, her voicemails, and her public comments never could.

She hesitates. She has been here before — or somewhere that looks like here. Another mechanism. Another channel through which her experience will travel into a system that has no particular obligation to receive it.

But this mechanism is different, not in how it feels when she submits it, but in what happens after.

Once submitted, her review is verified against ownership and published on the community's profile. It sits alongside the accounts of other verified homeowners, forming a record that is visible to buyers before they commit, to boards before they respond, and to the market that previously could not see any of it. It contributes to a governance score the board did not create and cannot dismiss. It remains.

She has not changed the system yet. She has become part of the signal that will.

The effort is identical. The outcome is not.

WHY THE BARRIER WAS NEVER THE PROBLEM

The common explanation for low homeowner engagement is apathy — the belief that people do not participate because they do not care. This explanation is convenient, and it is wrong.

The homeowner described here was not apathetic. She attended meetings, documented issues, and used every available channel. Others did the same in different ways. The failure was not the absence of engagement. It was the absence of return.

The mechanisms available to homeowners were designed for compliance, not consequence. They received input and acknowledged it, but they did not convert it into outcomes the homeowner could see, measure, or rely on. Over time, the pattern became clear. Effort did not produce proportional results.

That pattern changes behavior. Not because people care less, but because they learn what the system does with their effort.

If the problem were apathy, the solution would be motivation. If the problem is return, the solution is structural — a mechanism that produces an outcome proportional to the effort. The review is that mechanism. Not because it is easier, but because it produces a result.

WHAT ELEVEN MINUTES ACTUALLY PRODUCES

The eleven-minute review does not feel consequential when written. It feels like a small act — a few paragraphs describing something that has been happening for years.

What it produces is larger than its context.

At the community level, it becomes part of a record built from verified homeowner experience. Individual accounts aggregate into patterns, and patterns become governance history. That history does not disappear when boards change or management companies rotate. It persists as a record of what it was actually like to live there.

At the market level, it contributes to a benchmark that defines performance across comparable communities. It establishes context where none existed before.

At the decision level, it reaches people previous channels never could — buyers, lenders, realtors, and boards — before decisions are made.

The review does not enter the system that ignored it. It creates a different one.

WHAT PARTICIPATION SIGNALS

Participation itself is a signal.

A community with consistent participation signals engagement, visibility, and accountability. It tells the market that experience is being recorded and that governance is observable. A community without participation signals something else — not necessarily failure, but uncertainty. In a system where visibility is possible, the absence of it becomes information the market interprets.

Participation is not just input. It is evidence.

THE FIRST PERSON WHO MOVES

Every system that changes begins the same way. Someone acts before the outcome is guaranteed.

The first review does not change the system. It establishes that the system can be used. The second confirms it. The third begins to form a pattern. The system does not wait for scale to begin working. It begins working when participation starts.

The homeowner who submits the first review is not waiting for the system to exist. They are part of the condition that creates it.

WHAT HAPPENS IF YOU DON'T

The system will still move.

Other communities will participate. Their records will form. Their governance will become visible. Their buyers will have information your buyers do not. Their boards will receive feedback your board does not.

The difference does not remain neutral. It compounds.

The community that participates becomes understood. The community that does not becomes uncertain. In a market that can see, uncertainty is not invisible. It is priced.

THE SCALE THAT MAKES IT MATTER

One review is a data point. Ten reviews are a pattern. At scale, the signal becomes infrastructure.

The individual cannot see that scale while participating, but the system converts their input into something larger. Without the review, there is no signal. Without the signal, no benchmark. Without the benchmark, no standard.

The smallest action and the most important action become the same.

Eleven minutes. Honest. Specific. Submitted into a system designed to convert experience into consequence.

That is what changes everything.

CHAPTER 16

THE SYSTEM THAT CANNOT SEE ITSELF

Why the system isn't broken–it's blind–and how visibility turns hidden waste into billions in savings

He had served on the board for three years and considered himself a conscientious steward of the community's finances. He attended every meeting. He read the reserve study. He asked questions at vendor presentations. He voted to approve the management company's recommended budget each year, the recommended reserve contribution rate each year, and the recommended vendor contracts each year—because the management company was the professional in the room, and he was a retired schoolteacher who had volunteered for a role no one else wanted.

When the special assessment arrived—$5,800 per unit, due in ninety days—he was as surprised as anyone. The parking structure had failed. The reserve fund was insufficient. The remediation could not wait. He had voted on every decision that produced this outcome and had not known, at the time of any of those votes, that the outcome was accumulating.

He was not negligent. He was not corrupt. He was operating in a system designed, in every structural detail, to prevent him from knowing what he needed to know to govern well. More precisely: he was operating in a system with no external reference point—no comparable community against which his board's decisions could be measured, no benchmark against which the management company's advice could be evaluated. Without comparison, the accumulating cost was not just invisible. It was structurally unavoidable.

At the level of a single community, that dynamic is easy to miss. A homeowner experiences a single assessment. A board manages a single budget. Each decision feels contained, local, and specific to a single set of circumstances.

But the system is not local.

Across the United States, more than forty million homes are governed by associations of this type, representing roughly seventy-seven million residents. The combined value of those communities approaches eleven trillion dollars, and the annual cost to operate them exceeds $140 billion. These numbers are often presented as indicators of scale. They are more accurately understood as indicators of exposure.

Because when a system of that size operates without a mechanism to compare performance, the inefficiencies do not remain isolated. A maintenance decision made without reference to alternatives in one community is made again in another, and then again in thousands more. A reserve strategy that appears reasonable in isolation is replicated across portfolios without ever being evaluated against a benchmark. Each decision carries a marginal cost that is never measured in context.

Over time, those margins accumulate.

Estimates of that inefficiency—spread across maintenance practices, vendor selection, reserve misalignment, and risk pricing—reach into the tens of billions annually. Not because the system is dominated by bad actors, but because it has never required those decisions to be compared.

At that scale, even small inefficiencies are not small. They become structural.

This chapter is not about bad boards. It is about a system without a feedback mechanism—and what happens to every participant when a system cannot see itself.

THE DIAGNOSIS EVERYONE GETS WRONG

The conventional diagnosis of HOA failure is personnel. The board was incompetent. The property manager was dishonest. The vendor was unreliable. The homeowners were apathetic. Change the people, fix the problem.

This diagnosis is satisfying and wrong. It is satisfying because it assigns blame to identifiable parties and implies a solution—remove them and replace them with better ones. It is wrong because it mistakes the symptom for the cause. Incompetent boards, self-interested management companies, and underperforming vendors are not aberrations in the HOA system. They are the predictable output of a system that provides no feedback, no benchmark, and no mechanism that connects governance behavior to consequence.

Replace the board and the new board faces the same conditions. Replace the management company and the new one operates in the same information environment. The pattern persists not because the people are irredeemably flawed but because the architecture produces the same result regardless of who occupies it. The HOA system does not have a people problem. It has a feedback problem—and feedback problems are architectural, not personal.

WHAT A FEEDBACK MECHANISM DOES

Every well-functioning system has a feedback mechanism: a signal that connects outputs to inputs and tells the people making decisions whether those decisions are producing the intended result. A thermostat measures temperature and adjusts the furnace. A company reads quarterly earnings and adjusts strategy. A doctor reads vitals and adjusts the treatment. In each case, the feedback mechanism makes correction possible. Without it, the system continues in its current direction regardless of where that direction leads.

The HOA system has no such mechanism—and critically, it has no comparison. The board makes decisions and receives no external signal of whether those decisions are above or below what any peer community would produce. The management company advises and receives no verified account of how its advice is experienced compared to competing firms. The vendor performs and is measured against no benchmark it did not help establish. No comparison means no pressure. No pressure means no change. And no change means that the costs that should be prevented instead accumulate—quietly, predictably, in the structure of every budget cycle that passes without scrutiny.

THE BOARD'S STRUCTURAL DISADVANTAGE

The board member who approves a vendor contract, a reserve contribution rate, or a maintenance deferral is making a decision with less information than the party advising that decision. This is the board's structural disadvantage, and it is nearly impossible to overcome within the current system.

The management company knows how this vendor has performed in its other communities. The board does not. The management company knows what reserve contribution rates it has recommended across its portfolio and what the outcomes have been. The board does not. The management company knows the history of the maintenance request that was closed without resolution, the early warning that was noted and filed, and the complaint that was discouraged from becoming an external record.

This information asymmetry is not incidental. It is structural. When the management company's knowledge advantage is used in the community's interest, it produces good governance. When it is used in the management company's interest—to recommend the vendor that pays a referral fee, to advise the reserve rate that avoids uncomfortable budget conversations, to discourage external reporting that complicates the carrier relationship—it produces the outcome the retired schoolteacher did not see coming. The board cannot correct what it cannot see. And the board has no independent basis to ask whether what it is being shown is the full picture, because it has never seen another picture to compare it against.

This is not a conspiracy. It is an information environment that systematically disadvantages the party with the most accountability and advantages the party with the least.

THE PMC'S RATIONAL SELF-INTEREST

Property management companies are not, as a category, bad actors. They are organizations responding rationally to the incentive structure the system has built for them. The PMC is paid a flat management fee regardless of governance outcomes. Its contract limits liability for decisions it frames as board decisions. Its renewal depends on maintaining a functional relationship with the board, not on producing measurable improvements in community performance. The vendor relationships it manages generate referral income. The reserve rate it recommends is the one least likely to produce a difficult budget conversation.

None of these incentives requires bad intent. They require only that the PMC's financial interests not perfectly align with the community's—and in a system without a performance benchmark, that misalignment is invisible until the cost appears.

In two HOA communities where I have lived, one a mid rise and the other a high rise both over 25 years old two different management companies—the homeowners received the same instruction from both property managers when homeowners raised a concern about a common area condition: do not report it to the city. In focus groups conducted across the country during the research for this book, homeowners described the same experience unprompted, from Florida to Arizona to Chicago and South Florida. The language differed. The instruction was identical: do not file. It will affect our insurance.

The consistency of this instruction across geographies and management companies is not coincidence. It is the rational behavior of a party operating in a system where the cost of suppression falls on the homeowner and the benefit of suppression accrues to the manager—and where no external record exists to make the pattern visible.

The instruction was not advice. It was a signal. In a system without external visibility, the safest move for the manager is not to surface risk—it is to contain it. The cost of that containment does not disappear. It transfers, accumulates, and returns later as failure, assessment, or loss. The manager benefits in the present. The homeowner pays in the future.

THE HOMEOWNER'S IMPOSSIBLE POSITION

The homeowner in this system occupies the most information-rich position and the least structurally protected one. They see the water staining after the first heavy rain. They notice the elevator running rough for three months. They observe the pool deck crack that has been growing since last summer. They experience the maintenance request closed without resolution, the vendor whose repair requires a return visit within six weeks.

They see all of this before the physical inspection, before the reserve study, before the claim.

And then they are told not to file.

The homeowner who raises a concern at a board meeting is thanked and told the matter is being monitored. The homeowner who submits a maintenance request finds it closed without explanation. The homeowner who considers reporting a common area code violation is informed that doing so could affect the community's insurance coverage. The individual homeowner voice is not weak because homeowners don't care. It is weak because every channel through which it might be expressed is controlled by the party it is meant to evaluate. The maintenance request system, the board meeting agenda, the community newsletter, the annual survey—all of it flows through the PMC.

The homeowner is the most continuous observer of governance quality in the system. They are also the party least able to make what they observe matter. That is not an accident. It is the architecture.

WHAT A FEEDBACK MECHANISM CHANGES

The CTI™ does not fix the board. It does not reform the management company. It does not guarantee accurate reserve studies or fair insurance pricing. It does one thing: it introduces a feedback mechanism—and for the first time, a basis for comparison—into a system that has had neither.

The homeowner who submits a verified, anonymous CTI™ review describing a maintenance concern that was raised and not resolved, a management instruction to avoid external reporting, or a vendor whose repair required multiple return visits is producing governance intelligence in a channel the management company cannot control, edit, or suppress. That intelligence enters the permanent record. It is available to the board at contract renewal. It is available to the insurer at premium negotiation. It is available to the prospective buyer evaluating the community before making the largest financial decision of their life.

The board that reviews its CTI™ scores and discovers that maintenance execution is trending below peer communities, that communication scores have declined for three consecutive quarters, and that homeowner trust in the management company ranks in the bottom quartile of comparable firms has information it did not have before. A board that can see how its community compares does not ask whether it is satisfied—it asks why it is not doing better, and what the contract renewal conversation should look like. That is a different conversation. It produces different outcomes.

WHAT FEEDBACK CHANGES IN PRACTICE

A feedback mechanism does not change intent. It changes behavior.

When performance becomes visible and comparable, decisions are no longer made in isolation. They are made in context—against what other communities are doing, what other management companies are producing, and what outcomes are actually occurring over time. That shift—from isolated judgment to comparative evaluation—is where the economic impact begins.

COST

- Inefficiency is no longer repeated invisibly. When one community overpays for a vendor, underfunds reserves, or defers maintenance beyond what comparable communities sustain, that gap becomes visible—and once visible, it becomes difficult to justify repeating.

- Deferred maintenance is identified earlier, when intervention is less expensive and before it compounds into capital failure or insurance exposure.
- Insurance risk is surfaced before it becomes a pricing event, allowing the board to respond while options still exist rather than after the market has already reacted.
- Pricing that once relied on assumption begins to reflect actual performance, as decisions are made against observable outcomes rather than internal expectation.
- Costs that once accumulated quietly begin to surface while they are still manageable, reducing the likelihood of sudden, high-impact financial events.

PRODUCTIVITY

- The board no longer spends cycles debating incomplete information. It operates with directional clarity—what is underperforming, what is trending, and where attention is required.
- Management companies are no longer operating on internal knowledge alone. Their performance is reflected back through verified homeowner experience across time, narrowing the gap between what is reported and what is experienced.
- Vendor performance issues are identified and addressed with fewer cycles because they are no longer anecdotal—they are observable patterns.

Decisions begin to resolve issues the first time, rather than returning in cycles.

EFFICIENCY

- Practices begin to converge toward what works. Not because they are mandated, but because high-performing patterns become visible and repeatable across communities.
- Low-performing behaviors—whether in maintenance execution, communication, or vendor reliability—become increasingly difficult to sustain once they can be compared.
- Communities begin to operate against a benchmark rather than habit, reducing duplication of error and drift in decision-making.

The system reduces friction not by adding control, but by removing uncertainty.

The CTI™ does not reduce cost directly. It makes cost visible. And in a system where cost can be seen and compared, it does not remain elevated for long—because it can finally be challenged.

THE RESISTANCE

Property management companies will push back against the CTI™. The objections will come in predictable forms: the data is biased toward unhappy homeowners; the methodology lacks transparency; scores will be weaponized rather than used as signals. Each objection is addressable on its merits—verified ownership as a participation qualifier, twice-annual collection to reduce event-driven bias, anonymity to reduce retaliation risk, scoring against community benchmarks rather than absolute standards.

But the more important response is architectural. The CTI™ is not designed to be adopted by management companies. It is designed to be adopted by homeowners, boards, insurers, lenders, real estate agents and buyers—every party whose interests are served by governance visibility. The management company that performs well has nothing to fear from a verified performance record; it has everything to gain. A CTI™ portfolio showing strong scores across managed communities is a credential no competitor without the record can match. The management company that resists most vigorously has already answered the question the score would have asked.

THE SYSTEM THAT CAN SEE ITSELF

The retired schoolteacher was not a bad board member. He was a board member operating without a feedback mechanism—and without any external reference point—in a system designed to keep governance invisible to the people it affects most. The management company that advised him was, in all likelihood, acting in its own rational self-interest in a system that never required it to do otherwise. The homeowner who flagged the water intrusion and was told not to file made a rational calculation: speaking carried risk and produced no measurable outcome.

The system produced the special assessment. Not the people.

Across 77 million Americans living in common-interest communities, governing assets that approach $11 trillion in aggregate value, that dynamic repeats in every community that has never been compared to another—every board that has never had a benchmark, every management contract renewed because no one had a number to argue from. The CTI™ does not change the people. It changes the architecture. It introduces the comparison the system has always lacked: the signal that makes board decisions visible to homeowners, PMC performance visible to boards, and governance quality visible to the insurers and lenders and buyers who have been pricing it blind. The special assessment that arrives without warning is not a failure of memory or attention. It is what happens when no comparison was ever possible. That is where the cost lives—in the absence of the benchmark—and that is precisely where the CTI™ begins.

HOA failure is not a personnel problem—it is a feedback problem. A system that cannot compare itself cannot correct itself. The CTI™ introduces the benchmark that turns invisible, accumulating cost into visible, actionable signal.

PART III – THE SHIFT

When a system that can finally see itself begins to change–and the market responds

CHAPTER 17

THE LIABILITY ILLUSION

Why avoiding visibility feels safe–and why it creates the very risk it was meant to prevent

The warning existed.

It had been written down. It had been presented. It had been discussed in a room where the people responsible for acting on it were sitting — board members, a property manager, an attorney whose role was to advise on what the language required and what it did not.

The engineering report described structural deterioration. Waterproofing failure. Concrete damage that would expand if not addressed. The language was technical, specific, and clear enough that anyone reading it carefully would understand the direction the building was moving.

The direction was not good.

What happened next was not negligence in the way negligence is usually imagined — not a single moment where someone refused to act on something obvious, not a decision that appeared irrational at the time it was made. What happened was something more common and more consequential than a single bad decision.

The report entered a system that was not designed to act on it quickly. The cost of repair was significant. The process required coordination, approvals, and funding. The board needed time. The homeowners needed to be informed. The work needed to be scoped, bid, and scheduled. Each step was reasonable. Each delay was explainable. Individually, none of those decisions looked like failure.

Collectively, they were.

The system did not fail because someone made a bad decision. It failed because the structure prevented a visible one — and the attorney in the room, whose job was to protect the association, had spent years advising boards that visibility was the risk, not the absence of it.

THE LEGAL INSTINCT

The instinct to limit exposure is not irrational. Attorneys advising HOA boards operate within a framework built on a premise that is correct as far as it goes: what is written can be used, what is admitted can be argued, what is inconsistent can be exploited. The goal is to reduce the association's vulnerability in the event of a dispute.

That produces familiar guidance. Be careful what you document. Avoid statements that could be interpreted as admissions. Communicate through formal channels. Follow established process. Address concerns internally before they become external records.

This is not bad advice. It is correct advice — applied to the wrong problem. Because the problem the HOA system faces is not how to defend itself after something goes wrong. The problem is how to prevent what goes wrong in the first place. And a framework designed for the first problem, applied to the second, does not produce prudent governance. It produces the liability illusion.

DEFENSE VS. PREVENTION

Legal frameworks are designed for defensibility. They assume an event has already occurred — a claim has been filed, a dispute exists, a record is being reconstructed in the direction most favorable to the client. The objective is to limit what can be proved and minimize what must be paid. That is a legitimate objective in its proper context.

HOA governance operates in a different time horizon entirely. The most important decisions are made before anything goes wrong — when a maintenance issue is first identified, when a reserve shortfall begins to develop, when a pattern of delayed response starts to emerge across homeowner requests. These are not legal moments. They are operational ones. The system that treats them as legal moments — that filters early warnings through a framework of documentation risk and admission exposure — is applying a defensive posture to a window that requires action.

The system has confused these two-time horizons for fifty years. It has applied a defensive framework to a preventive problem. And the result is not a community that is better protected from liability. It is a community that has traded the ability to see its own trajectory for the appearance of legal discipline — while the conditions that will eventually produce the claim continue to develop, undisturbed, in the space the reduced visibility created.

THE LIABILITY ILLUSION

Reducing visibility does not reduce risk. It removes early signals. This is the liability illusion — the belief that limiting what is written, keeping issues contained within controlled channels, and avoiding records that could later be used in a legal context constitutes risk management. It feels prudent. It feels disciplined. It feels like the kind of careful governance that protects the association.

It is not. Because the underlying conditions do not change when the records about them do. Concrete continues to deteriorate whether or not it is discussed openly. Water intrusion continues whether or not it is escalated externally. Maintenance delays continue whether or not they are aggregated into a visible pattern. What changes is the system's ability to see those conditions early enough to act on them — and early action is the only intervention that changes the cost.

The arithmetic of deferred maintenance is the clearest expression of what the illusion actually costs. A waterproofing repair identified when a homeowner first reports staining in a storage unit costs $18,000 — a manageable capital expense, fundable within the normal budget cycle, addressable before the summer construction season ends. The same repair, filtered through a system that acknowledges the report, closes the ticket as internally managed, and defers the external inspection for two budget cycles, costs $95,000 as an emergency remediation — plus the special assessment required to fund it, plus the homeowner whose unit was damaged in the interim, plus the insurance claim that now sits in the loss history at the next renewal. The liability illusion saved the association from a written record. It cost the association $77,000 and a claim.

Suppressed reporting follows the same pattern at a longer interval. A homeowner identifies a structural concern and raises it at the board meeting. The property manager thanks them and explains that the reserve study has not flagged the area as a near-term priority. The homeowner raises it again six months later. The property manager advises against filing a complaint with the city building department, explaining that an external inspection could affect the community's insurance coverage. The homeowner does not file. The condition continues to develop. Two years later, a section fails. The remediation costs $340,000. The carrier pays the claim and issues a non-renewal notice. The record the system worked to suppress does not disappear — it reappears in the loss history, in the engineering report reconstructed after the failure, in the deposition of the homeowner who raised the concern twice and was told twice to stay quiet.

What is not recorded is not resolved. It is deferred — at compound interest.

THE COST OF SILENCE

Silence does not eliminate the record. It delays it, and it concentrates what arrives when the delay ends.

The sequence is consistent enough to constitute a pattern. A homeowner identifies a condition — a crack, a leak, an elevator running rough for three months, a waterproofing membrane that looks different after the first heavy rain. The condition is raised. It is acknowledged. It is not escalated, because escalation creates a record, and the system has been trained to treat records as exposure. The condition develops. It crosses the threshold from maintenance issue to capital event at a moment nobody in the system can identify precisely — because the system was not watching. The failure arrives, and with it the record the system spent years avoiding: the claim, the remediation estimate, the reconstruction of every decision made in the interval between the first report and the failure.

The legal system is exceptionally good at reconstructing that record. What it cannot do is create visibility before the events that make reconstruction necessary. The cost of silence is not the absence of liability — it is the concentration of it. The claim that arrives after a suppressed condition has developed for two years is larger than the claim that would have arrived after an addressed condition was resolved in two months. The insurance premium that follows the claim is higher. The special assessment required to fund the remediation is larger. The trust that erodes when homeowners learn the system had early warning and chose to manage it quietly is not recovered by a newsletter.

The record does not disappear. It reappears at the moment it is most expensive — in the form the legal framework was designed to manage rather than the form that could have been prevented.

THE SHIFT

A system that cannot see itself cannot correct itself. The missing element in HOA governance has never been information — the information exists, distributed across homeowner observations, maintenance logs, reserve studies, and the engineering reports that arrive too late to change outcomes that were already forming. What has been missing is the structure that organizes those fragments into a signal early enough to act on.

The verified homeowner review system is that structure. Not because it replaces the legal framework or removes the attorney from the governance equation — the attorney's role remains essential, and the board that governs without legal counsel is taking a different kind of risk. What changes is the information environment in which that counsel operates. The attorney advising a board that has access to a verified, recurring signal of its own governance trajectory is advising a client that can see what it is producing before the failure arrives. The defensive posture that made sense when the alternative was no signal at all makes less sense when the signal exists and the board has chosen not to read it.

From suppression to structured visibility. A system that can see its own trajectory behaves differently than one that cannot — not because the people inside it changed, but because the information environment they are governing from changed. That is what the standard provides. Not a constraint on governance. A window into it.

WHAT SMART COUNSEL WILL DO

The role of legal counsel does not disappear when the governance signal exists. It evolves — from managing the record after a claim to structuring the governance environment that produces fewer claims to manage.

The attorney who understands what the verified homeowner signal reveals will use it as the early warning instrument it is. A maintenance execution score that has been declining for four consecutive quarters is not a legal document. It is a pre-legal signal — the condition that will become a legal document if the board does not act on it. The counsel who reads it as a liability indicator, who brings it to the board as evidence of a governance trajectory requiring correction, is performing the risk management function the traditional defensive model claimed to perform while actually deferring the risk forward.

Standardized maintenance response protocols reduce inconsistency — and inconsistency, documented across verified homeowner accounts, is the pattern that produces the enforcement discrimination claims the defensive model was designed to defend against. Clear financial communication reduces the ambiguity that produces special assessment disputes. Proactive vendor accountability reduces the deferred maintenance that produces the structural failures that produce the claims. The attorney who helps a board build these practices is not abandoning the defensive framework. They are applying it earlier — at the point where it can prevent the event rather than manage its aftermath.

The role of counsel evolves from limiting exposure to structuring the governance environment that reduces what needs to be limited.

THE INFLECTION POINT

For decades, boards could operate within a system where visibility was optional and the absence of a verified record felt like protection. That condition is changing — not through regulatory mandate, not through legislative reform, but through market pressure that is redefining what the absence of visibility signals to every party evaluating a community from the outside.

Buyers are asking different questions. The buyer who searches a community's CTI™ record before scheduling a showing is asking questions the disclosure package was never designed to answer — and the community that has no record is not presenting as a clean slate. It is presenting as a community that has chosen not to be seen. Insurers are evaluating governance behavior alongside loss history, and the community whose homeowners consistently describe suppressed reporting and deferred maintenance is a community whose underwriting conversation is changing regardless of whether a claim has been filed. Lenders are expanding their view of community risk to include the governance conditions that predict financial instability — and the community without a verified governance record is a community the lender cannot evaluate.

The question that board chairs are beginning to hear from their own sellers — the homeowners whose units are sitting on the market while comparable communities move — is the question that changes behavior faster than any bylaw revision or state statute: why are we the only ones not participating?

That question has an answer the legal framework cannot provide. The attorney who advises the board to remain invisible because visibility creates exposure is advising a client that the market is beginning to price as exactly what the attorney was trying to avoid — a community with something to hide.

The HOA system did not lack warnings. It lacked a mechanism that made those warnings impossible to ignore — that converted the homeowner's observation into a permanent, verified, publicly accessible record that neither the board nor the management company could manage into silence.

For fifty years, the system attempted to reduce risk by reducing visibility. It produced the conditions that made the claims it was designed to defend against more likely, more expensive, and more concentrated than they would have been in a system that could see itself coming.

The system can now see itself. The attorney who built a practice on managing the record after failure will find that the record is no longer the association's to manage — it is being built, continuously, by the verified homeowners who live inside the governance the board is producing. The risk was never absent. It was unobserved.

That condition has changed. And the counsel who understands what that means will have already told their clients.

The liability illusion protected the record. It did not protect the building. The system that reduces visibility to manage its legal exposure does not eliminate risk — it removes the early signal that would have allowed the risk to be managed before it became a claim. The record does not disappear. It reappears at the moment it is most expensive. That is what the verified governance signal changes: not who is liable after the failure, but whether the failure was visible early enough to prevent it.

CHAPTER 18

THE BUYER'S NEW PLAYBOOK

What the home search looks like when the community is finally visible

The offer was ready.

She had spent four months searching. She had walked through thirty-one properties in nine neighborhoods. She had lost two offers to competing bids and withdrawn a third after an inspection revealed a foundation issue the listing had not disclosed. She was tired in the specific way that serious buyers get tired — not discouraged, but worn down by the gap between what the process promised and what it consistently delivered.

The fourth offer felt different. The unit was right — the layout, the light, the way the kitchen connected to the living space in a way that matched how she actually lived. The neighborhood was right. The price, after two rounds of negotiation, was right. The inspection came back clean. The school district rating was strong. The walkability score was posted directly in the MLS listing, alongside the property tax history and the HOA dues amount.

And this time, there was something else on the listing page.

A number. 4.4 out of 5. Five colored bars beneath it, each representing a dimension she had never previously been given the tools to evaluate. A link that opened into verified homeowner narratives — specific, calm, detailed in the way that only people who have lived somewhere for years can be detailed.

She read for twenty minutes. Then she made the offer.

Not because the 4.4 guaranteed anything. Because for the first time in four months of searching, she understood what she was buying into. Not just the unit.

The community. The governance. The financial trajectory. The daily experience of the people already inside it.

Before this, buyers saw the home. Now they see the system.

WHAT THE SEARCH USED TO COST

REVISED: Section retitled from "WHAT THE SEARCH USED TO LOOK LIKE" to foreground cost rather than description — consistent with prosecutorial register

For the first fifty years of the HOA era, the home search had a structural blind spot that nobody named because everybody assumed it was unavoidable.

A buyer could see everything about the property. Price history. Square footage. Renovation details. Inspection reports. Flood zone designation. School district ratings. Crime statistics. Proximity to transit. The MLS had developed, over decades, into a comprehensive information environment for evaluating the physical and locational attributes of a home.

What it could not show was the community the home sat inside.

The HOA disclosure package — the stack of documents that arrived late in escrow, formatted for legal compliance rather than buyer comprehension — contained fragments of the picture. Reserve study projections. Budget line items. Meeting minutes that described decisions without context. Governing documents that ran forty pages and assumed a working knowledge of HOA law to interpret.

A sophisticated buyer with time, patience, and professional guidance could assemble those fragments into something approximating a governance picture. Most buyers did not have all three. And even the sophisticated buyer was assembling the picture from documents produced by the institution being evaluated — the financial statements prepared by the management company, the meeting minutes approved by the board, the reserve study commissioned by the association.

The picture was drawn by the subject of the portrait.

Disclosure requirements exist for good reasons. The problem is not that disclosure exists. The problem is that disclosure cannot produce the signal a buyer needs at the moment they need it — a verified, standardized, comparable account of what living in this community is actually like, derived from the people who have been doing it.

That absence had a cost. The buyer who closed without it paid — sometimes immediately, in the form of the special assessment the reserve study had been predicting for three years, and sometimes slowly, in the form of the governance environment they had committed to without being able to evaluate it. For fifty years, that cost was invisible because the instrument to surface it did not exist. The buyer absorbed it as bad luck, or bad timing, or the inevitable friction of a complex transaction.

It was neither bad luck nor bad timing. It was a structural condition the market had never been required to correct.

REVISED: Added final paragraph converting descriptive section into argument about structural cost of absence — consistent with Part I register

THE FIVE QUESTIONS THE SCORE ANSWERS

The CTI™ composite score answers five questions the prior disclosure environment could not answer clearly, quickly, or comparably. Not because it replaced the reserve study or the financial disclosure — those documents remain the authoritative record. Because it produced, for the first time, a verified account of what those documents meant in practice for the people who lived inside them.

REVISED: Added "Not because" clause to clarify the CTI™ is a complement to existing documents, not a product replacement pitch

The first is governance consistency. Is this community governed fairly? Are the rules applied to everyone, or selectively? Is the board making decisions that reflect the interests of the homeowners it serves? Before the CTI™, a buyer had no way to answer this before closing. They would find out the way every homeowner finds out — by living inside the enforcement pattern long enough to recognize whether it was consistent or not. The governance dimension score answers the question in advance, drawn from the verified accounts of homeowners who have been watching the board operate for years.

The second is financial health trajectory. Not whether the reserves are technically adequate today, but whether the community is moving toward adequate funding or away from it. A reserve study showing 67% funding is a data point. What the buyer needs to know is whether that 67% reflects consistent, deliberate funding practice or a fund that was at 80% three years ago and has been declining as the board prioritized dues stability over reserve adequacy. The financial stewardship dimension score answers the trajectory question in a form the reserve study percentage alone cannot.

The third is maintenance reliability. Not whether the property looks well-maintained in listing photos, but whether maintenance issues are addressed consistently when they arise. A property that looks beautiful in March listing photos may look different in October after a summer of deferred maintenance requests. The buyer who reads the maintenance execution score evaluates the community at its typical operating moment — not its best presentation moment.

The fourth is communication quality. Whether the homeowner is kept informed of decisions before they produce consequences. Poor communication is the force multiplier of every other governance failure. A special assessment preceded by months of transparent communication about reserve trajectory is a fundamentally different experience than one that arrives detached from any visible history.

The fifth is the one no financial document can answer: do the people running this community actually serve the people living in it? Emotional trust is the dimension most resistant to institutional manipulation. A board that meets every procedural standard while conducting its actual business in ways that exclude, intimidate, or disadvantage homeowners will score poorly here. The governance documents will not show it. The homeowners will. For the first time, governance risk has a number.

Emotional trust is also the leading indicator that every other dimension eventually follows. Communities where homeowners trust their board identify and address governance problems before they compound. Communities where that trust is absent accumulate problems in the dark — and the special assessment that eventually arrives is the visible terminus of an invisible failure the emotional trust score had been signaling for years.

HOW THE BUYER READS THE SCORE

The CTI™ composite score is a starting point, not a conclusion. The buyer who sees a 4.4 and stops reading has used the score as a triage mechanism — legitimate and valuable, but incomplete.

A composite of 4.4 built on consistent 4.5s across all five dimensions is a different community than a composite of 4.4 built on a 4.9 in emotional trust and a 3.2 in financial stewardship. Both produce the same headline number. Their trajectories are different. The first is performing consistently across every dimension. The second is warm and trusted — and financially vulnerable in a way the composite alone conceals.

The buyer who reads the dimension breakdown walks away informed. They know to pull the reserve study. They know to ask specifically about the capital improvement history. They know to read the financial stewardship narratives, where verified homeowners have described, in their own words, the specific decisions and patterns that produced a 3.2 on the dimension that matters most to their long-term investment security.

The verified homeowner narratives are where the score becomes human. The numerical dimensions tell the buyer what the community is producing. The open text comments tell them what it feels like to live inside it. Reading enough verified narratives across enough communities builds a literacy about governance quality that no disclosure package has ever produced. Buyers learn to distinguish between a community whose negative comments cluster around a single issue and one whose negative comments describe a governance culture. The difference between a problem and a pattern.

THE PRICE CONVERSATION CHANGES

The signal changes what the buyer can say at the negotiating table — not because it gives buyers leverage, but because it gives the negotiation a basis it has never previously had.

REVISED: Opening sentence reframed from "The CTI™ score does not just change what the buyer knows" — removed product-forward framing, replaced with consequence framing

Before the verified governance signal existed, price negotiation in HOA communities was conducted against the physical attributes of the property. Inspection findings produced repair credits. Appraisal gaps produced price adjustments. The governance condition of the community was not part of that conversation — not because it was irrelevant to price, but because it had never been quantified in a form a negotiating buyer could put on the table.

A financial stewardship score of 2.8 in a community with a three-year-old reserve study is a quantified signal. The buyer who presents it at the negotiating table is presenting something that did not exist in prior transactions: a verified, standardized assessment of the governance risk they are being asked to absorb at the listed price. The seller's agent who dismisses it has to explain why the verified accounts of current homeowners should be discounted in a price negotiation about the long-term value of a home in that community.

This does not produce automatic price reductions. It produces a specific, documentable basis for a negotiation that governance risk has always deserved and never previously received.

THE OFFER THAT DIDN'T HAPPEN

The clearest measure of what the verified signal changes is not the transactions it informs. It is the ones it prevents.

The buyer who reads a financial stewardship score of 2.6 in a community with a three-year-old reserve study and a deferred capital improvement list visible in the open text comments has been handed information the prior disclosure environment did not produce until after closing. They can walk away before spending sixty days on a transaction built on incomplete information. They can negotiate a price that reflects the risk. What they cannot do is proceed uninformed.

The offers that don't happen because a buyer read the score and walked away are not market failures. They are the market functioning correctly. The buyer avoided a cost. The seller lost a transaction because their community's governance record was publicly visible — and goes back to the board with a message it has never previously been required to receive: our record is costing us buyers.

The board that receives that message from one seller can dismiss it. From five sellers in the same quarter, it is a market verdict. Market verdicts change behavior in ways that bylaws, statutes, and certification programs have not.

REVISED: Replaced "The CTI™" with "the verified signal" and "a buyer read the CTI™" with "a buyer read the score" — removes product-name repetition that reads as marketing; the argument is about the signal, not the brand

THE BUYER SHE BECAME

She closed on the unit. The 4.4 had held through the due diligence process — no surprises in the reserve study, no gaps in the financial record, no maintenance narratives that contradicted what the score described. The board had governed with the same core team for four years. The management company had maintained an above-benchmark maintenance execution score across three consecutive review cycles.

She moved in on a Saturday. The following Tuesday, a weekly community update arrived — maintenance completed the prior week, requests received and their status, the upcoming board meeting agenda, and a brief note about a parking structure sealant project on track with the timeline the board had communicated six months earlier.

She read it in ninety seconds. She did not attend the board meeting. She did not need to. She knew what was happening in her community. She had known before she moved in. She had known before she made the offer.

The community is visible now. And a buyer who can see it will not buy into one they cannot.

CHAPTER 19

THE BOARD THAT DECIDED TO LEAD

What high-performing governance actually looks like – and what separates the boards that get there from the ones that don't

She had been on the board for fourteen months when the report arrived.

She had not asked for it. The quarterly summary had been generated automatically — a report showing the community's composite score, its dimension breakdown, and the market comparison that showed where the community stood relative to comparable communities in the same zip code.

She almost didn't open it.

She had joined the board because a neighbor asked her to. There was a vacancy. She had time. She thought she could contribute something. She was not a professional property manager, an attorney, or a financial analyst. She was a homeowner who paid dues every month and believed, in the uncomplicated way that people believe things before they are tested, that the community she lived in was well-run.

The report showed her otherwise. Not dramatically. Not in the way that suggests fraud or catastrophe. In the quieter, more consequential way that shows a system drifting — a maintenance execution score that had been declining for six quarters, a communication score that had never been high, an emotional trust dimension sitting at 2.9 in a market where comparable communities averaged 3.8.

She read the report twice. Then she called the board chair.

He told her the scores reflected a small number of unhappy homeowners. He told her every community had them. He told her the methodology was unproven, and that the board had been governing this community well for years. One report was not going to change that.

She listened. She thanked him. She hung up.

Then she called the next board meeting to order and put the report at the top of the agenda.

WHAT SEPARATES THE BOARDS THAT LEAD

Every HOA community has a board. Not every HOA community has a board that leads.

The distinction is not about credentials. It is not about hours logged or sincerity of intent. Most boards are composed of genuinely well-intentioned neighbors who volunteered to serve and would be surprised to learn the impact their decisions produce. Intent is not the variable that separates the boards that lead from the ones that drift.

The variable is accountability. Specifically, accountability to a standard that exists outside the board's own judgment of itself.

The board that measures its performance against its own history — against the absence of a major crisis, against the fact that dues are collected and the lights are on — is not governing. It is maintaining. Maintenance preserves the current condition. Governance improves it. Communities that confuse them drift in the direction that unmeasured systems always drift: toward the path of least resistance.

Most boards aren't failing. They're measuring themselves against nothing.

The board that leads has found a way to see itself from the outside. It has access to a reference point it did not set and cannot revise. It governs not against its own sense of its history but against an empirical account of what comparable communities are actually achieving.

Give a board a mirror and they manage their appearance. Give them a window and they manage their performance.

This is not a small distinction. A board governing from internal metrics — management company reports, annual meeting attendance, the absence of visible crisis — is governing from a signal the institution largely produces for itself. A board governing from verified homeowner experience, compared against a market benchmark it did not design, is governing from a signal that cannot be manufactured in its favor. The information environment determines the governance quality. Boards can only act on what they can see.

THE FIVE PRACTICES OF HIGH-PERFORMING BOARDS

Across communities that consistently score in the upper range of the benchmark, five practices appear with enough consistency to constitute a pattern. They are not complicated. They are not beyond the reach of any volunteer board willing to adopt them. They are what governance looks like when a board has decided to lead rather than maintain.

REVISED: Removed "CTI™" from "upper range of the CTI™ benchmark" — the benchmark is the reference point, not the product; consistent with prosecutorial register where the mechanism is on trial

The first is proactive financial communication. The high-performing board does not wait for the annual meeting to communicate the community's financial condition. It communicates continuously — in plain language, through channels homeowners actually use, before decisions are made rather than after their consequences arrive.

The board that announces a dues increase at the annual meeting and explains the reserve trajectory that made it necessary is governing differently than the board that sends the same announcement without context. The outcome is identical. The experience is not. The homeowner who understood the trajectory before the increase arrived experienced it as the expected conclusion of a conversation they were part of. The homeowner who received the increase without context experienced it as an imposition from a system they were not part of. Over time, the accumulation of unexplained outcomes is precisely what the emotional trust dimension measures and what drives it below benchmark.

Proactive financial communication is not complicated. It is a newsletter paragraph. It is a one-page reserve summary included with the monthly statement. It is the board chair who opens the annual meeting by spending five minutes explaining where the reserve fund stands and what the current contribution rate is doing to close or widen the gap. None of this requires professional financial training. It requires the decision to communicate before the consequence arrives.

The second is consistent, documented enforcement. Enforcement inconsistency is the single most common governance failure in HOA communities, and the failure that produces the most lasting damage to emotional trust. The homeowner who receives a violation notice for something unenforced against their neighbor does not experience that notice as governance. They experience it as targeting.

The high-performing board does not eliminate violations. It applies them consistently. Every enforcement decision is documented. Every variance from standard practice is explained in writing. Every homeowner who receives a violation notice receives it through a process identical to the one applied to every other homeowner in the same situation. This is not a high standard. It is the minimum standard for a governance system that expects the people it governs to trust it.

The third is vendor accountability through independent verification. The high-performing board uses verified homeowner feedback as a check on management company reporting — not as a replacement for it, but as an independent signal the management company did not produce and cannot revise.

When the maintenance execution score declines for three consecutive quarters and the management company reports that vendor performance is satisfactory, the gap between those two signals is not a data anomaly. It is a question. The board that governs from both signals — and knows how to read the gap between them — is the board that cannot be managed by its own management company.

The fourth is structured homeowner engagement. The high-performing board does not wait for homeowners to show up at meetings. It creates structured mechanisms for homeowner input that do not require attendance at a two-hour weeknight meeting.

This is a governance design problem, not a technology problem. The board that asks homeowners a specific question receives information it can act on. Structured engagement produces a signal. Unstructured engagement produces noise. The homeowner who is asked a specific question and sees evidence that the answer influenced a board decision is a participant. The homeowner who submitted a comment at the annual meeting and never heard about it again is a witness. Participation sustains governance quality. Witnessing allows it to drift.

The fifth is external benchmarking. The high-performing board does not evaluate its performance against its own history. It evaluates its performance against the market. The board that opens the quarterly report, sees the market comparison, and asks what the communities scoring above us are doing differently has chosen to govern rather than maintain. That choice, made every quarter, is the practice that separates the boards that lead from the ones that drift.

THE BOARD CHAIR WHO CHANGED HIS MIND

She put the report at the top of the agenda, and the board chair pushed back.

He was not a bad board chair. He had served the community for six years. He had managed crises, navigated difficult homeowners, and shepherded the community through a major roof replacement that required a special assessment nobody wanted. He had earned his sense of the community's condition through years of direct engagement with its problems.

What he had not done was see the community from the outside.

She presented the report carefully. Not as an accusation. As a question. The maintenance execution score had declined for six consecutive quarters. The emotional trust dimension sat at 2.9 in a market where comparable communities averaged 3.8. These were not one homeowner's opinion. They were the pattern across every verified homeowner who had submitted a review in the community over the past eighteen months.

She asked: what would we need to change to close that gap?

The board chair was quiet for a moment.

He had been asking the wrong question for six years. He had been asking whether the community was better than it had been — whether the major problems were resolved, whether the homeowners who attended meetings were satisfied. Those were answerable questions. They had been answering them, and the answers had been acceptable.

The question she was asking was different. Not whether the community was better than it had been. Whether it was as good as it could be. Not whether the homeowners who attended meetings were satisfied. Whether the homeowners who didn't attend — the majority, the ones who had adapted, disengaged, and stopped expecting the system to respond — were experiencing a community worth being part of.

He picked up the report. He looked at the maintenance execution section. He looked at the pattern — response times lengthening for two years, requests being closed without resolution, a gap between what the management company was reporting and what the homeowners were experiencing.

He had known about individual complaints. He had not known they were the same complaint, repeated across the community, pointing to a systemic failure in how maintenance was being executed. Individual complaints were manageable. A systemic pattern was a governance problem.

He set the report down.

He said: let's start with maintenance.

Four words. No fanfare. That sentence was the governance inflection point — not a resolution, not a policy, but a decision to start from what the homeowners were reporting rather than from what the management company was.

WHAT CHANGES WHEN THE BOARD DECIDES TO LEAD

The board that decides to lead does not transform overnight. The score does not jump from 3.1 to 4.4 because a board chair changed his question. Deferred maintenance does not resolve in a quarter. Homeowners who disengaged three years ago do not re-engage because the board sent a newsletter.

What changes immediately is the information environment the board is governing from. The board reading the quarterly report — comparing its dimension scores to the market benchmark, tracking each dimension's trajectory over time, using the homeowner narrative to identify the specific patterns producing the scores — is governing from a fundamentally different position than the board relying on management company reports alone.

The management company reports what it managed. The homeowners report what they experienced. The board that reads both — and governs from the gap between them — is the board that can ask the questions the management company's reports were never designed to answer.

Those questions drive the specific changes that move the score. The maintenance execution score declining for six quarters produces a focused investigation: which vendor, which request category, which response timeline is producing the pattern? The question is answerable with the data. The answer produces an action. The action produces a result. The result appears in the next review cycle.

Enforcement consistency produces the slowest score movement because it requires the most sustained behavioral change. The board that has been applying rules unevenly for three years does not produce consistent enforcement in a quarter by deciding to. It produces consistent enforcement by building the documentation practices and the reporting structure that makes consistency possible to maintain across board member transitions and management company changes. That infrastructure takes time to build. The score reflects it when it is built.

Over time, as the board acts on what it sees — as maintenance response times shorten, as enforcement becomes consistent, as financial communication improves, as homeowners begin to re-engage because engagement is producing results — the score moves. Not because the board wanted a higher score. Because the board improved the governance the score was measuring.

The community that earns its score did not do it by chasing a number. It did it by deciding, at some point, to stop measuring itself against nothing — and to start measuring itself against the honest account of what the homeowners it serves are experiencing every day.

A board that chases the score produces the appearance of improvement. A board that improves the governance produces the score.

CHAPTER 20

THE CONTRACT YOU NEVER READ

How HOA management agreements quietly transfer risk, limit accountability, and shape your community

She had been asking the same question for eleven months.

Not aggressively. Not through an attorney. She sent emails. She attended meetings. She submitted the maintenance request twice, then a third time with photographs. She asked the property manager directly. She raised it at an open board forum. Each time, she was told the matter was under review, then that it had been forwarded to the vendor, then that the vendor had been asked to re-evaluate, then that the board would take it up at the next meeting.

The next meeting came. The item appeared on the agenda under Other Business. A board member moved to table it pending additional information. The motion passed. The homeowner drove home in eleven minutes.

She was not angry. She was confused. There were professional people managing her building. There was a contract. There was a board with fiduciary obligations. There was a vendor who had performed the original work, an insurance carrier, a reserve study, and a property management company that had been in place for six years.

She asked her neighbor — a retired commercial litigator — why nobody could give her a direct answer about a $4,000 repair.

He thought about it for a moment.

"Because," he said, "giving you a direct answer is the one thing every layer of this system has been contractually structured to avoid."

THE DOCUMENT THAT RUNS THE COMMUNITY

Most homeowners know their community has governing documents. CC&Rs. Bylaws. Rules and regulations. They may not have read all of them, but they understand these documents exist and that they matter. What most homeowners do not know is that a second document often shapes the daily experience of the community just as much — and almost no one ever sees it.

The management contract.

In most HOA communities, the management agreement defines who handles maintenance requests, who coordinates vendors, who prepares budgets, who communicates with homeowners, who manages reserve reporting, and how problems move through the system when they arise. It is, in practical terms, the operating manual for how the community functions day to day.

Most homeowners could request it. Most do not know to ask.

The contract operates in the background — invisible until a lawsuit, a major assessment, or a structural failure forces someone to read what was actually agreed to. And when homeowners finally do read it, the picture is almost always different from what they assumed.

The management company appears to sit at the center of operations. It handles communications. Vendors report to it. Maintenance requests flow through it. Financial reports carry its name. From every visible angle, it looks like the party responsible for outcomes.

The contract says otherwise.

Most management agreements contain extensive language narrowing liability and protecting the company from claims connected to board decisions, vendor actions, reserve shortfalls, construction outcomes, or maintenance failures outside a carefully defined list of duties. The company coordinates. The board decides. The vendor executes. The attorney advises. Each layer participates — and each layer is shielded by a contract that limits how much of the outcome it can be held responsible for.

That is not fraud. It is architecture.

The problem is that homeowners are living inside the architecture without knowing it exists.

THE GAP BETWEEN INFLUENCE AND ACCOUNTABILITY

One of the most disorienting experiences in HOA life is watching responsibility move.

A project goes wrong. The homeowner begins tracing accountability backward. The board approved it. Management coordinated it. The vendor performed it. The engineer reviewed the scope. The attorney advised on the contract language. The prior board had deferred related maintenance. Insurance was notified. Inflation affected costs. Supply chain issues affected timing.

Every statement may be partially true. None of them answers the question.

This is the defining feature of modern HOA governance: operational influence can be very high while formal accountability remains very narrow. The management company that recommends every vendor, coordinates every project, prepares every budget, and drafts every homeowner communication is not, under most contracts, legally responsible for the outcome of those decisions. The board that approves those recommendations often lacks the technical expertise to evaluate them independently. The vendor limits future responsibility through warranties and exclusions. The attorney reduces exposure without operating the property.

When all of those protections stack inside one system, accountability becomes nearly impossible to locate — not because someone is concealing it, but because the structure was designed to distribute it until it disappears.

The homeowner experiences one community. One roof. One reserve fund. One monthly payment. One set of consequences.

The system experiences itself as a network of separate legal and contractual relationships, none of which holds the whole.

That gap does not stay abstract. It shows up in language.

A direct answer becomes a carefully worded answer. A carefully worded answer becomes a procedural update. The procedural update goes through legal review. Legal review narrows the language further. The homeowner receives a response that technically addresses the question while leaving the core concern exactly where it was.

Most homeowners eventually name this experience the same way.

"I can never get a straight answer."

They assume it is a communication failure. It is a structural one. Every layer of the system has been organized to respond without resolving — to acknowledge without admitting — because clear admission, in any form, is precisely what every contract in the stack was written to prevent.

THE MEETING AFTER THE MEETING

Most homeowners believe decisions happen during meetings.

That belief is understandable. Agendas are posted. Board members sit at the front of the room. Motions are made. Votes are recorded. From the outside, the process looks open enough that residents assume they are watching decisions form in real time.

They are usually watching the final stage of a process that ended somewhere else.

By the time most significant issues reach a public agenda, the operational direction has often already been shaped through management recommendations, vendor conversations, legal review, and informal board discussions that occurred before the meeting opened. Some of this is operationally necessary — complicated projects cannot be understood for the first time in front of a room full of homeowners. But the effect on residents is consistent regardless of intent.

They arrive to participate. They leave having observed.

Over time, that distinction changes behavior. Homeowners stop attending because they no longer believe attendance changes outcomes. Boards interpret the empty chairs as satisfaction. Silence gets read as stability. A community can register nearly zero visible conflict while trust erodes steadily underneath the calm surface of monthly meetings and approved minutes.

The withdrawal is almost never dramatic. A homeowner skips a meeting. Then another. Stops reading the board packet. Stops submitting maintenance concerns because prior submissions produced acknowledgment but not resolution. Still pays dues. Still waves to neighbors. Still lives inside the community — but has emotionally separated from the governance process surrounding it.

The disengaged homeowner and the satisfied homeowner look identical from the outside. Both are quiet. Both are present. Both appear in the attendance data the same way: absent.

Most HOA systems are not designed to distinguish between them.

The vendor ecosystem reflects the same structural logic. In many communities, the same contractors appear repeatedly across years and across management portfolios — not necessarily through improper arrangement, but through the compounding inertia of familiarity. Familiar vendors know the property. They understand HOA administrative requirements. Boards feel safer approving them. Over time, the formal bidding process can become a structured confirmation of a conclusion that was largely reached before the proposals arrived. Homeowners see the vendor selected and the project announced. The recommendation process that preceded the announcement happened in the same invisible space as everything else: the meeting after the meeting.

WHAT PERFORMANCE HAS NEVER BEEN MEASURED AGAINST

Most HOA communities renew management contracts based on habit.

Not negligence. Habit. The contract comes up for renewal. The relationship is familiar. The system is still functioning. No catastrophic failure has forced a reexamination. The board votes to continue.

What almost never happens is a structured assessment of whether the homeowner experience over the contract period matches the operational responsibilities the agreement was supposed to deliver. Response times are not benchmarked. Communication quality is not scored. Vendor oversight is not evaluated. Homeowner confidence is not tracked. The gap between what the contract promised and what residents experienced stays invisible — not because anyone conceals it, but because no mechanism has ever existed to surface it.

The CTI™ is that mechanism.

Not a complaint system. Not a referendum. A verified, recurring, anonymous record of governance behavior from the people who experience it every day — scored across the dimensions that determine whether a community is being operated transparently, responsively, and in the long-term interest of the homeowners paying into it.

When CTI™ scores show sustained communication distrust, declining maintenance execution, or accelerating homeowner withdrawal, those are not expressions of sentiment. They are operational signals — the same patterns that precede special assessments, insurance disruptions, vendor disputes, and board recalls, now legible months or years before pressure becomes crisis.

The management company that has renewed on habit for eight years has never had to answer the question the CTI™ makes unavoidable: does the verified experience of this community match the contract we signed?

For most of HOA history, that question had no answer because homeowner experience had no structure. Frustration stayed fragmented across private emails, hallway conversations, and isolated board meeting comments that never connected into a pattern visible enough to act on. The homeowner who stopped participating left no record. The homeowner who gave up asking questions left no signal. The community absorbed the withdrawal quietly because no instrument existed to measure what was being lost.

The CTI™ does not predict whether a roof will fail or whether reserves are adequately funded. Engineering does that. Reserve specialists do that. What the CTI™ introduces is behavioral visibility — a structured record of how governance is actually experienced by the people living inside it, produced continuously, before the pressure that makes records unavoidable has arrived.

Not after the recall. Not after the lawsuit. Not after the assessment lands and homeowners are reading the management contract for the first time, trying to reconstruct how eleven months of unanswered questions about a $4,000 repair produced consequences that everyone in the building could feel coming.

Before.

The management company signed a contract. The CTI™ is the first mechanism that tells you whether they kept it.

CHAPTER 21

THE MANAGEMENT COMPANY RECKONING

What happens to the industry when performance becomes visible at scale

The email arrived on a Tuesday morning.

He had been running the regional office for nine years. Forty-three communities. Eleven managers. A portfolio that had grown steadily through acquisition and referral, built on the relationships that property management had always run on — board members who trusted the company, developers who recommended it, attorneys who knew the principals. The business model that had worked for two decades in this market.

The email was from a board chair he had known for six years. A community the company had managed since its founding. A relationship he would have described, until that morning, as solid.

The board had reviewed the company's verified performance data across its portfolio. The maintenance execution scores had been below the market benchmark for four consecutive quarters. The communication dimension had declined in eleven of the forty-three communities over the same period. The emotional trust scores in three communities had dropped to a level the board chair described, carefully and without accusation, as concerning.

The board was putting the management contract out for competitive bid.

What the board chair did next had never been possible before. He searched management companies in the region — not by referral, not by reputation, not by the recommendation of the developer who built the community or the attorney who drafted its governing documents, but by verified homeowner performance data, filtered by geography, community type, and portfolio size.

He filtered by maintenance execution score. Then by emotional trust. Then by the trajectory of both over the preceding eight quarters — because a company whose scores were climbing told a different story than a company whose scores were static or declining, even if the current numbers looked similar.

He could see how individual managers performed across the communities they personally managed. The manager who had overseen five communities and maintained above-benchmark scores in all five was visible. So was the manager whose scores had declined in every community they had touched.

The board was no longer hiring a company and hoping for the right manager. It was hiring with the ability to ask, specifically, who would be assigned to this community and what their verified performance record showed.

The management company that had always won contracts through relationships was now competing against companies whose relationships were with their scores.

THE INDUSTRY THAT RELATIONSHIPS BUILT

The professional HOA management industry was built on relationships. This is not a criticism. Relationships are how trust is established in any service industry, and trust is what a board is purchasing when it signs a management contract. The board that trusts its management company governs differently than the board that does not — more confidently, more efficiently, with less friction and more focus on the decisions that matter.

But relationships also insulated the industry.

The management company that maintained strong board relationships did not need to demonstrate performance by any standard external to those relationships. The board that trusted its management company renewed the contract. Concerns were raised through the relationship — through the conversation with the account manager, through the annual review meeting, through the informal channels that had always been the primary mechanism of feedback in an industry that had never developed a formal one.

The board knew whether it trusted its management company. It did not know whether that trust was warranted. For fifty years, no mechanism existed to answer that question from the outside.

The verified homeowner signal changes that condition. Not by attacking relationships — a relationship informed by accurate performance data is a stronger relationship than one built on trust without verification. What changes is the basis on which trust is extended. The management company that earns renewal from a position of demonstrated performance holds that contract more securely than the one that holds it through inertia. The board that can verify whether its trust is warranted governs differently than the one that cannot.

REVISED: Replaced "The CTI™ opens the system" paragraph — removed product-forward framing, replaced with structural argument about what changes when trust can be verified

THE THREE COMPANIES

Three distinct responses to the verified performance signal are emerging, each producing a different outcome for the communities they serve and the market they compete in.

***REVISED: "CTI™ signal" → "verified performance signal"** — removes product-name repetition in favor of the mechanism*

The first is the company that leads with the signal. This company was performing well before the signal existed. Its homeowners were having good experiences. Its maintenance was responsive. Its financial communication was clear. Its boards trusted it not because they had no alternative but because the service it delivered consistently justified that trust.

What the verified record gives this company is something it could not produce for itself: proof. High scores across its portfolio are not self-reported. They are not produced by a certification program the company joined or a trade association the company belongs to. They are the verified account of the homeowners who live in the communities it manages — people whose ownership has been confirmed and who have no incentive to say the company performs well unless it does. This company leads with the record in every new business conversation. Self-reported excellence is a claim. Verified excellence is a competitive advantage.

The second is the company that uses the signal to improve. This company was performing adequately — managing communities well enough that contracts renewed and the business continued to grow through the relationships that had always driven it. The verified benchmark reveals that adequate is not the same as competitive. This company identifies the specific dimensions where its performance lags, traces those dimensions to the operational practices producing them, and changes the practices. The trajectory changes — and in a market where buyers, boards, and lenders are increasingly consulting verified performance data, trajectory matters as much as current position.

The third is the company that cannot see what the signal is telling it. This company has built its business on practices the verified record makes visible in ways that are uncomfortable — preferred vendor relationships that direct community spending toward contractors whose primary qualification is their relationship with the management company, portfolio sizes that make genuine community knowledge impossible, communication practices that satisfy reporting requirements without producing homeowner comprehension.

None of these practices are necessarily illegal. Many are standard across the industry. The companies that built their businesses on them did not do so with malicious intent. They did so because the industry rewarded efficiency and relationship continuity, and these practices produced both. The verified record measures what they cost. The response that attributes scores to factors outside its control, questions the methodology, and continues the practices is the more common one. It is also the one that ends contracts steadily, as boards that once had no alternative discover they now have several.

THE CONSOLIDATION THAT CREATED THE PATTERN

The consolidation of the professional property management industry over the past two decades was rational from a financial perspective. The margins on individual community contracts are thin. Profitability at scale requires managing many communities efficiently. The business model that optimized for efficiency — centralized service platforms, standardized processes, portfolio sizes that maximized manager utilization — was the business model that attracted investment and grew.

It was also the business model that replaced community knowledge with process and relationship depth with relationship breadth. The manager who knew a community's specific history, its recurring issues, its board dynamics, its particular homeowner personalities, was replaced by a manager handling thirty communities from a centralized platform. The local vendor relationships that produced cost competition were replaced by preferred vendor networks that produced cost consistency — which is not the same thing and does not serve the same interest.

These changes were invisible to the boards that approved them because the contracts looked the same before and after consolidation. The same services. The same monthly fee. The same reporting cadence. The board that had been satisfied with the company before acquisition had no reason to expect the service to change — and no mechanism to measure whether it had.

The homeowners knew. They experienced the distance increase as the consolidation moved through their portfolios. They felt the maintenance response times lengthen. They noticed when their manager became less familiar, when institutional knowledge was replaced by ticket numbers, when the person who answered the phone no longer knew their building's specific history.

They told their neighbors. They complained at board meetings. They wrote letters that were received and filed. None of that produced a signal the market could read. None of it was visible to the next buyer, the next board, the next management company evaluating whether to acquire the portfolio.

The verified homeowner record is that signal. The communities that experienced the service change are now describing what they experienced in permanent, publicly accessible reviews. The pattern is visible — not in any individual community's story, but in the aggregate picture that emerges when enough communities managed by the same company describe the same experience in the same terms. The consolidation that was invisible while it was happening is visible now.

WHAT THE RECKONING LOOKS LIKE

He called his operations director. She had been expecting the call.

They spent three hours with the data. Not the individual community scores — he had seen those. The patterns across the portfolio. The maintenance execution decline tracked precisely with the portfolio expansion that had followed the acquisition eighteen months earlier. The communication scores dropped in every community where the platform changeover had replaced personal manager contact with automated response systems. The emotional trust scores correlated almost perfectly with the communities where manager turnover had been highest in the preceding two years.

He had known the acquisition had been disruptive. He had not known it was producing a consistent, measurable, publicly visible decline in homeowner experience across nearly a third of his portfolio. Individual complaints were manageable. A systemic pattern mapped across forty-three communities was a different kind of problem — one that required a different kind of response.

He called the board chair back. Not to defend the scores. To share what the data had shown him and describe what he was going to change.

The acquisition had expanded the portfolio faster than the company's operational infrastructure could absorb. Manager-to-community ratios had increased. The platform changeover had been implemented on a timeline driven by the acquisition schedule rather than by readiness. Those were operational decisions. They had produced operational consequences that the homeowners had experienced and the verified record had captured.

He described the specific changes: manager reassignments to reduce portfolio load in the communities where emotional trust scores were lowest, a rollback of the automated response system in favor of direct manager contact for maintenance escalations, and quarterly performance reviews built into every board meeting agenda going forward.

The contract was not terminated. It was restructured — with quarterly performance reviews built into the terms, benchmarks tied to the market average, and a clear understanding on both sides that the relationship would be evaluated going forward by a standard neither party had invented and neither could revise.

That is what accountability looks like when it arrives in an industry that has operated without it. Not punishment. Structure. The structure that makes performance visible. The structure that makes improvement measurable. The structure that makes the relationship between the management company and the community it serves something more than an arrangement sustained by inertia and the absence of alternatives.

He hung up. He turned to his operations director.

She was already pulling the portfolio data.

CHAPTER 22

THE REALTOR'S MISSING SIGNAL

How real estate professionals have been advising clients without the most important piece of community intelligence – and what changes when it arrives at the listing level

She had been selling real estate for seventeen years.

She knew her market. She knew the neighborhoods, the school districts, the flood zones, the HOA communities that sold quickly and the ones that sat. She knew which developments had been built by developers who cut corners and which had not. She knew the difference between a listing that looked good and a listing that was good.

Seventeen years of transactions had given her a calibration that no certification program had ever replicated.

What she did not know — what seventeen years had never given her the tools to know — was what her clients were actually buying into when they bought into a managed community.

She knew the dues amount. She knew the amenities. She knew the rules around rentals and pets and exterior modifications — or thought she did, having developed the habit of skimming CC&Rs for the provisions that came up most often and trusting that the ones she skimmed past were unlikely to matter.

Sometimes they mattered.

The buyer who moved in and discovered the rental cap was lower than she had planned to use. The buyer who installed the pergola and received the violation notice three weeks later for a modification prohibited in language on page thirty-one that nobody had fully read. The buyer who was told the community was pet-friendly and discovered that pet-friendly meant one dog under twenty-five pounds and her two dogs did not qualify.

These were not failures of intent. They were failures of access. The information existed. It was in the documents. It was simply not organized in a form the transaction process made practical to use.

And behind the CC&Rs — deeper than the rules, more consequential than the pet weight limits and the parking restrictions — was the question she had never been able to answer at the moment it mattered most.

Is this a good community to live in?

Not a good building. Not a well-located development with reasonable dues. A good community. The kind where the board governs fairly and the management company delivers and the reserve fund is on a trajectory that protects her client from the assessment she will not see coming until it arrives. The kind where the people running the community take their responsibility seriously enough that the homeowners inside it describe the experience as one of being served rather than subjected.

She had instincts about that question. Seventeen years of instincts. She could walk into a building and feel the difference between a well-run community and one accumulating problems beneath a presentable surface.

But instinct is not a signal. It is a substitute for one.

She had been advising clients for seventeen years without the signal that would have made her instincts specific, verifiable, and comparable. She had not known it was missing because it had never existed.

Then it did. And when it arrived, it did not arrive as a new platform to learn or a new search to run.

It arrived in the MLS.

THE DISTINCTION THAT CHANGES EVERYTHING

The real estate profession has never lacked tools. It has lacked signals.

A tool requires the person using it to know what to look for, where to find it, and how to interpret what they find. The tool is only as good as the expertise of the person holding it. The agent with seventeen years of experience uses the tool better than the agent with three. The buyer with financial training reads the reserve study better than the buyer without it.

A signal is different. A signal is information the market produces and organizes into a form that anyone can read, regardless of prior expertise. The school district rating is a signal. The walkability score is a signal. The flood zone designation is a signal. Each of them democratizes information that was previously accessible only to experts — and each of them now appears, as a matter of course, on the listing page where every buyer and every agent begins their evaluation.

The HOA community has never had its equivalent. Not because the information was unimportant. Because the information did not exist in a form the MLS could carry.

Every signal that changed how buyers evaluate homes arrived on the listing page. Not in a separate tool. Not behind a separate search. On the listing page, where the decision begins.

The community governance signal is arriving the same way.

Price per Sq Ft. Days on Market. Walk Score®. CTI™. Four numbers. One of them is new. It is the one that tells you what it is actually like to live there.

THE FIELD THAT MARKETS PRODUCE

Every market that has developed a verified performance signal has eventually produced a standardized field through which that signal travels — not because someone designed the field in advance, but because the market created the condition that required it.

When enough communities had verified homeowner records, a question the listing page had never been required to answer became the question every buyer was asking: what does the score say?

The field that carries the answer is brand neutral by design. It belongs to the transaction — to the buyer who deserves the information, the agent who needs to provide it, and the market that has been operating without it. Any verified, third-party homeowner performance signal that meets the condition the market has established — ownership verification, independence from the institutions being measured, anonymity by default, standardized dimensions, public accessibility, recurring update cycle — can populate it.

The field is not a product. It is what the listing page looks like when the market has learned to require accountability.

That condition has a name: the Association Performance Indicator™. It is to HOA community governance what the school district rating is to education quality — the point at which information the market always needed, but could never previously organize, becomes the field the listing page was always missing.

What the field displays follows from what the market requires: the composite score, the five-dimension breakdown, the trajectory over eight quarters. The board score and management company score displayed separately — each derived independently from verified homeowner accounts, weighted equally, because the market's accountability interest extends to both governance and execution and the field that cannot distinguish between them cannot direct correction of either.

The community with a board score of 4.7 and a management company score of 2.6 has strong governance and weak execution. The board is making sound decisions. The management company is not implementing them. For a buyer, this profile's problems are fixable — a board committed enough to score 4.7 is likely already aware of the gap.

The community with a board score of 2.4 and a management company score of 4.3 is the opposite and a fundamentally different risk. The management company is executing well. But the board governing the community is producing a score its homeowners describe as unfair, inconsistent, and operating without transparency. The management company's professionalism cannot compensate for the governance decisions the board is making. This profile's problems are structural — they live at the governance level the management company cannot reach.

The realtor who can explain this distinction to a buyer is providing analysis that no prior signal made possible. Not because the realtor is smarter. Because the signal now exists on the listing page where the analysis begins.

WHAT THE SIGNAL CHANGES IN THE TRANSACTION

The arrival of the governance signal at the listing level does not add steps to the transaction. It moves information earlier — and the earlier timing is the specific change that matters, because information that arrives before a decision is useful and information that arrives after a decision is a wound.

Before the signal, governance risk entered the transaction late. It appeared in the disclosure package that arrived in escrow, formatted for legal compliance rather than buyer comprehension. It surfaced in the inspection, which measured the physical condition of the unit but could not measure the governance condition of the community surrounding it. It arrived, sometimes, as the lender's pause — the moment when financial records that had been sitting in a filing cabinet all along were finally assembled into a picture that changed what could be financed.

After the signal, governance risk enters the transaction at the first showing — before the offer, before the inspection, before sixty days of financial and emotional investment in a community whose governance record is already public and has been since the last review cycle. The buyer who reads the score before scheduling a showing is making a different decision than the buyer who discovers the same information thirty days into escrow.

The showing that starts with the signal produces different questions. The buyer who has read the verified homeowner narratives asks about the capital improvement history because the financial stewardship score told her to look there. She asks about the management company transition because the emotional trust trajectory told her something changed eighteen months ago. She asks about the enforcement history because the governance score sits below the market benchmark and she wants to understand why before she commits, not after.

Each question is specific because the signal made it specific. Specificity is what protects the buyer. Specificity is what the profession has always owed its clients and has never previously been equipped to deliver.

THE CONVERSATION THE PROFESSION HAS NEVER HAD

There is a conversation buyers deserve to have with their agents before making an offer on a home in a managed community. It has rarely happened because the agent did not have the information required to have it honestly.

Before the governance signal existed at the listing level, the agent who wanted to address community quality was reduced to instinct and generality. The community seems well-run. The financials look okay. These are honest statements. They are not signals. They are the professional equivalent of a shrug — an acknowledgment that the information required to be specific did not exist.

After the signal arrives on the listing page, the conversation is specific. The community you are considering has a composite of 4.2 in a market where comparable communities average 3.8. Its board score is 4.4 and its management company score is 4.0 — both above benchmark. Its financial stewardship trajectory has been stable for six quarters. The community two blocks away also has a unit meeting your criteria. Its composite is 3.1. Its board score is 2.4. Its financial stewardship trajectory has been declining for four consecutive quarters.

These are two different purchases. The unit is similar. The community is not.

That conversation protects the buyer. It also protects the agent. The realtor who had access to verified community performance signals at the listing level and did not use them is making a professional choice that will be harder to defend as the standard becomes the expectation.

THE TUESDAY AFTERNOON SHE OPENED THE LISTING

She pulled a listing on a Tuesday afternoon between showings. The address was a community where she had three active listings and one pending transaction. She had pulled this listing dozens of times. She knew the dues amount, the amenity package, the parking situation, the pet policy.

This time there was a new field on the listing page.

Association Performance Indicator™: 3.1. Below the market average of 3.8 for comparable communities in this zip code. Board score: 2.4. Management company score: 3.8. Financial stewardship trajectory: declining four consecutive quarters.

She read for eight minutes. Then she called her pending buyer.

Not to deliver bad news. To deliver information. The kind that arrives before the consequence rather than after. The kind that protects the person receiving it rather than the transaction producing it.

The kind she had been trying to provide for seventeen years without the signal to make it specific.

The signal was on the listing page now. Where it had always needed to be. Where every buyer would see it before they fell in love with a unit in a community they did not yet understand.

The profession does not get smarter when the signal arrives on the listing page. It gets specific. Specific is what the profession has always owed its clients and has never previously been equipped to deliver.

CHAPTER 23

THE INSURANCE RECKONING: PRICING BEHAVIOR

What carriers have never been able to price, why the PMC conflict makes it worse, and how verified homeowner intelligence changes the risk equation

The claim had been building for three years.

Not because anyone planned it. Because the conditions producing it had been accumulating — visible to the people closest to them, undocumented and unaddressed in the specific way that governance failures accumulate when no one in the system has both the standing to report them and the protection to do so honestly.

The parking structure had been flagged informally twice. First by a homeowner with twenty years in commercial construction who recognized the water intrusion pattern in the northeast corner as the early signature of rebar corrosion. He raised it at a board meeting. The property manager thanked him and explained the reserve study had not identified the area as a near-term priority. He raised it again six months later. The property manager told him that filing a formal complaint with the city building department would trigger an inspection that could affect the community's insurance coverage and potentially result in fines passed on to homeowners.

He did not file.

The second flag came from a homeowner directly above the affected section. She noticed staining on the ceiling of her storage unit. She submitted a maintenance request. It was closed with a notation that the area had been inspected and no active leak was present. She was not told what the inspection found, who conducted it, or that another homeowner had raised the same concern six months earlier.

Fourteen months later, a section of the parking structure ceiling failed. No injuries. The remediation cost was $340,000. The carrier paid the claim — then issued a non-renewal notice at the next policy anniversary.

The underwriting review found deferred maintenance, an inadequate reserve contribution rate, and a structural failure in the loss history. What it did not find was the homeowner who had flagged the problem two years before the failure, been discouraged from reporting it externally, and watched his maintenance request get closed without resolution.

The carrier prices the loss. It cannot price the decisions that produced it.

WHAT CARRIERS ARE ACTUALLY PRICING

HOA master policy underwriting rests on three data sources: physical inspection, loss history, and reserve study summaries. Each has the same structural limitation. It measures the past. Physical inspection measures the building at the moment the inspector walked through it, during a visit the community prepared for. Loss history measures events that have already occurred and been reported. Reserve studies reflect the financial position at the date of the study, commissioned by the association and reviewed by the association's own governing parties.

None of these sources measures governance behavior. None captures the decision-making culture that determines whether the physical assets will be maintained over the policy period. None reveals whether the board is creating liability before the liability event occurs. None shows whether the management company is suppressing the early warnings that could prevent the claims the carrier will eventually pay. The carrier is pricing the building. The risk lives in the governance.

Governance has been invisible to every underwriting model in the industry because no verified, standardized signal of governance behavior has existed at the community level. The CTI™ closes this gap by adding what the existing sources cannot provide: a verified, recurring, anonymous account of governance behavior from the people who experience it every day. Not the building — the decisions being made about the building, and the people responsible for making them.

THE GOVERNANCE RISKS CARRIERS CANNOT SEE

Five specific governance risk categories are surfaced by verified homeowner intelligence and invisible to conventional underwriting.

The first is fiduciary failure at the board level. Board members owe a fiduciary duty to the homeowners they serve — adequate common area maintenance, reserve funding that protects against foreseeable capital needs, consistent enforcement, and financial decisions made through transparent processes. When boards fail these obligations, they accumulate fiduciary liability that the carrier's D&O policy will eventually be asked to cover. The CTI™ governance dimension score is the earliest available signal of that failure — quarters or years before it arrives in a claim filing. The carrier that reads it is reading fiduciary exposure, not homeowner sentiment.

The second is preventative maintenance failure. Common area deterioration rarely arrives without warning. Water intrusion, structural fatigue, mechanical wear, and surface degradation all present early indicators that experienced observers recognize long before they become insurable events. When those indicators are identified and not acted upon — because the reserve study did not flag the area, because the vendor relationship did not incentivize early intervention, or because the board lacked the institutional urgency to authorize work outside the normal budget cycle — the cost of inaction compounds. Preventative maintenance is the difference between a managed cost and an insurable event. The CTI™ maintenance execution scores track whether communities are operating on the proactive side of that line or the reactive one.

The third is common area risk suppression. Common areas are where risk becomes shared — and where small failures become collective liability. There is a meaningful distinction between delay and suppression. Delay is the condition where a reported problem moves slowly through a system — acknowledged, assigned, and eventually addressed. Suppression is the condition where a reported problem is actively discouraged from entering the system at all — where the homeowner is told, directly or indirectly, that creating a record will produce consequences. In two HOA communities where I have lived — two different states, two different management companies — I received the same instruction from the property manager when I raised a concern about a common area condition: do not report it to the city. In multiple focus groups conducted across the country during the research for this book, homeowners described the same experience — unprompted, independently, in markets from Florida to Arizona to the Pacific Northwest. The language differed. The instruction was identical.

Do not file. It will affect our insurance.

This instruction matters specifically because common areas are shared assets whose deterioration creates shared liability. When a homeowner with relevant expertise identifies deterioration and is discouraged from creating an external record, the carrier is denied the early warning that could have prevented the claim it will eventually pay. What gets suppressed becomes what gets paid. The CTI™ anonymous review system breaks this pattern — the homeowner told not to file can describe that instruction in a verified, anonymous review without fear of retaliation.

The fourth is management practice exposure. PMC contracts position the management company as an agent executing board decisions. The board decides. The PMC executes. That framing limits PMC liability — and it is legitimate when it accurately describes the relationship. It does not always accurately describe the relationship. The management company that recommends vendors based on relationship rather than performance, that advises a reserve contribution rate below what the reserve study requires, that instructs homeowners not to report common area concerns externally — in each case, the contract language does not describe what happened. CTI™ scores show what the management company actually does. The gap between the contract language and the verified homeowner record is where E&O exposure lives — and where the carrier has been blind.

The fifth is insurance placement risk. In many HOA markets, insurance is not bid competitively. The management company that has placed community coverage with the same carrier through the same broker for eight years is not necessarily placing coverage that serves the community's current risk profile. The CTI™ financial stewardship scores signal whether the board is treating insurance procurement as the fiduciary decision it is, or allowing the management company to manage the relationship on terms that serve the management company's interests.

Minutes Are the Forecast

A reserve study describes the condition of a building. Meeting minutes describe the character of the people governing it.

That distinction is not academic. Reserve studies estimate remaining useful life, projected replacement costs, and funding recommendations based on a physical assessment at a fixed point in time. They tell you what the building needs. What they cannot tell you is whether the governance structure surrounding that building will respond — or defer, delay, and vote to revisit the question next quarter.

The elevator that requires replacement within three years is information. The board that has tabled the elevator discussion across four consecutive meetings is a pattern. The reserve study reveals the first. The minutes reveal the second. The carrier prices neither.

Most catastrophic HOA claims do not arrive without warning. They arrive after a long sequence of decisions — individually defensible, collectively disqualifying — in which a known maintenance obligation collided with political difficulty, financial discomfort, or vendor inertia and lost. A project postponed pending additional bids. A reserve increase deferred to protect dues stability. An engineering recommendation received, discussed, and tabled without action. Each decision entered the minutes. None of it entered the underwriting model.

This is the gap the CTI™ closes. Repeated communication distrust, declining maintenance scores, homeowner withdrawal from participation — these are the behavioral precursors to structural failure, and they surface in verified homeowner data months or years before they surface in a claim filing. The carrier reading CTI™ maintenance execution scores across eight consecutive quarters is not reading homeowner sentiment. It is reading the governance behavior that determines whether a deferred condition becomes a managed repair or a $340,000 remediation and a non-renewal notice.

Two communities can present identical physical inspection results, identical loss histories, and identical reserve summaries while operating with fundamentally different governance cultures. One surfaces problems early, funds repairs before they compound, and maintains the kind of homeowner trust that produces accurate, continuous risk intelligence. The other tables, defers, and suppresses — until the loss forces the issue into public view.

For decades, carriers have had no mechanism to distinguish them. The verified record is that mechanism.

THE HOMEOWNER AS RISK DETECTOR

Every HOA insurance carrier is missing the same resource: the verified, anonymous account of the homeowner who sees the common area risk before it becomes the claim. Inspections are scheduled. Reserve studies are periodic. Loss history is, by definition, retrospective. Each of these sources captures a moment in time. None captures the interval between those moments — the weeks and months when conditions are developing, early indicators are visible, and the window for preventative action is still open.

Homeowners are the most continuous risk observers in the system. They walk the parking structure every day. They notice the water staining after the first heavy rain. They observe the elevator running rough for three months. They see the pool deck crack that has been growing since last summer. They experience the maintenance request closed without resolution, the vendor whose repair requires a return visit within six weeks, the common area lighting that has been inadequate since the wrong fixture was installed. They see all of this before the physical inspection. Before the reserve study. Before the claim.

The homeowner is not the weakest signal in the system – they are the most continuous one.

The homeowner with twenty years of commercial construction experience who recognizes rebar corrosion in a parking structure is carrying insurance-relevant information no physical inspector would find on a scheduled annual visit. In the current system, most of what they observe stays private — submitted through maintenance request systems the PMC controls, raised at board meetings where the response is to thank them and note the issue is being monitored, or abandoned after the instruction to stay quiet.

The CTI™ anonymous review system creates the channel that does not currently exist. The homeowner who submits a verified review describing a common area maintenance concern that has been raised and not addressed, or a property manager instruction to avoid external reporting, is producing insurance-relevant documentation in a permanent, verified, publicly accessible record. The CTI™ does not create this layer. It organizes it.

The anonymous protection is not incidental to this function. It is essential to it. The homeowner told that reporting a common area code violation to the city could affect the community's insurance coverage is being offered a specific inducement to stay silent. The only mechanism that overcomes that inducement is the guarantee that speaking will not produce retaliation. The homeowner told to look the other way on a common area hazard has been carrying insurance-relevant information the carrier has never been able to access. The anonymous review is the channel that finally gets that information where it needs to go.

REWARDING PREVENTION

The most consequential change that verified governance data produces in HOA insurance is not better risk pricing at renewal. It is a premium incentive structure that rewards the governance behavior preventing claims rather than pricing the history of claims already paid.

The current model prices history. A clean loss record produces a lower premium. That is actuarially rational — and structurally backward-looking in a way that creates no incentive for governance improvement before a loss occurs. The community that prevents a structural failure through proactive maintenance and responsive homeowner engagement receives the same premium treatment as the community that defers maintenance until the failure occurs, as long as neither has filed a claim yet.

Verified governance data changes the actuarial basis for differentiation. The carrier that can distinguish the community whose maintenance execution scores show consistent, proactive common area maintenance over eight consecutive quarters from the community whose scores show deferred responses, suppressed early warnings, and declining homeowner trust has the basis for a premium structure that prices governance behavior rather than loss history alone. That structure creates the incentive the HOA system has never had: a direct financial reward for the practices that prevent the claims the carrier would otherwise absorb. The board that governs transparently, funds reserves adequately, and maintains common areas proactively is building the verified record that reduces the community's insurance premium — connecting governance quality to homeowner cost in the most direct terms available.

The community that prevents claims has always existed. What has never existed is the insurance premium that recognizes it.

WHAT THE VERIFIED RECORD CHANGES AT RENEWAL

For decades, communities have entered insurance renewal conversations with the same information set: loss history, reserve study summaries, and a project questionnaire. Each tells the carrier what happened. None tells the carrier what is happening — how decisions are being made, whether maintenance issues are being surfaced early or suppressed, whether the board is treating reserve funding as a fiduciary obligation or a dues-stability calculation.

A community with a documented, multi-period verified governance record enters that conversation differently. It can show how it operates, not simply what it has avoided. That distinction matters in underwriting because it moves the pricing conversation from retrospective to prospective — from what has been paid to what is likely to be paid next.

For Directors and Officers underwriting, sustained governance scores provide evidence of consistent fiduciary practice over time. Board decisions that are poorly documented, inconsistently applied, or resistant to homeowner input are the conditions that produce D&O exposure. A multi-period governance record is the earliest available signal of that exposure — or its absence.

For property and master policy underwriting, maintenance execution scores indicate whether a community is managing physical assets proactively or deferring against them. Multi-period consistency in these scores supports the argument that loss concentration — the tendency of deferred conditions to surface as large, sudden claims — is less likely in this community than in one with no observable maintenance history.

For general liability underwriting, participation rates and communication scores indicate whether hazards are being surfaced early or suppressed. A community where homeowners actively participate and communication is clear and timely presents a different incident profile than one where participation is low and reporting is discouraged.

For umbrella and excess underwriting, the longitudinal record shows whether issues are being identified and contained or allowed to accumulate over time — the layer of information that has historically been unavailable to severity assessment.

Property management companies occupy a specific position in this shift. A management company with access to verified governance data across its portfolio can identify risk patterns early, bring objective performance evidence into board conversations, document the execution that carriers need to see, and align reserve funding with the conditions that actually drive claims. That is proactive risk management — and the management company that operates at this level is not simply reducing liability for individual communities. It is influencing how those communities are priced, and distinguishing itself in a market where governance quality is becoming observable for the first time.

Brokers representing well-governed communities have always known they were bringing a better risk to the table. The verified record gives them the documentation to prove it — and gives carriers the structured basis to price that difference rather than assume equivalence across communities that look similar on paper but operate very differently in practice.

Insurance has always priced outcomes. Verified governance data introduces the ability to price behavior.

The carrier prices the loss. The verified governance record prices the decisions that produce it — and the community that builds that record is the community the carrier can finally distinguish from the one that cannot.

CHAPTER 24

THE LENDER'S NEW CALCULUS

From borrower risk to systemic risk

She was a loan officer in Phoenix, and she had learned to read the moment a file changed.

Not the moment a borrower's credit shifted or an appraisal came back short. Those were legible. What she had learned to read was subtler — the moment midway through underwriting when the community surrounding the borrower stopped looking stable. A reserve study three years stale. A special assessment levied eight months before the purchase. An insurance renewal that had increased 40 percent with no explanation in the HOA minutes. She had started keeping a list. Not of borrowers who failed to qualify. Of borrowers who qualified — and of what arrived six months later.

The list was long. And it had nothing to do with the borrowers.

The numbers are not subtle. Homeowners association and condominium fees have risen sharply across the country, with increases exceeding 25% since 2019. Monthly costs that were once manageable have moved into a range that is now influencing purchase decisions, refinancing decisions, and long-term affordability.

These increases are not being driven by discretionary upgrades. They are being driven by structural pressures that have been building for years and are now surfacing simultaneously. Insurance costs have reset higher. Deferred maintenance is no longer deferrable. Regulatory requirements are forcing stronger reserve positions. A lender reviewing a file today may find a borrower who qualified comfortably two years ago facing a materially different cost environment — not because the borrower's situation changed, but because the community's did. In some cases, a special assessment arrives between origination and close, recalculating what the borrower can comfortably carry. The file that looked clean at submission looks different thirty days later.

The result is not just higher monthly fees. It is unpredictability. Homeowners are no longer able to assume that costs will remain stable. Special assessments are appearing with little warning. Large capital projects are being accelerated. The financial profile of a community can change quickly, and when it does, the borrower absorbs the impact regardless of individual financial discipline.

In focus groups conducted with homeowners across multiple markets, a recurring theme has emerged: residents are not only feeling financial pressure — they are reconsidering whether to stay. The calculus is shifting from "can I afford this home" to "can I afford this community." When affordability pressure reaches this level, it does not stay contained to individual decisions. Residents who can leave begin to. Turnover increases. Owner-occupancy ratios shift. Demand softens in communities where costs have become unpredictable. What began as a household-level concern becomes a market signal. Affordability pressure becomes system risk when it repeats at scale.

Unpredictability is what lenders price as risk.

For decades, lenders have relied on relatively stable assumptions about the communities surrounding the borrower. Project-level risk was present but limited, and often secondary to the borrower's financial profile. That assumption is now being challenged. A borrower may qualify on paper. Income, credit, and debt ratios may align with underwriting standards. But the environment surrounding that borrower is no longer stable in the way it once was. The association itself may introduce volatility that was previously difficult to detect or quantify. This is the beginning of a structural shift. Lending is moving from a borrower-only model to a broader view that includes the stability of the community itself. The question is no longer just whether the borrower can repay the loan. The question is whether the system surrounding that borrower supports predictable repayment over time.

THE INFORMATION GAP CONVENTIONAL UNDERWRITING CANNOT CLOSE

For decades, mortgage lending has centered on the borrower. Credit score, income, debt-to-income ratio, employment stability, and down payment have formed the foundation of underwriting decisions. These inputs are structured, comparable, and widely understood. The community surrounding the borrower has also been considered, but in a limited and binary way. Associations are reviewed for basic eligibility: minimum reserve funding, acceptable owner-occupancy ratios, absence of significant litigation, and compliance with project guidelines. These checks are important, but they are static. They answer whether a project meets a threshold, not how it is performing over time.

What this model does not capture is variation within approved communities. Two associations can both meet minimum requirements while operating at very different levels of effectiveness — one proactive and transparent, the other reactive and under pressure. A community in Scottsdale and a community in Tempe may carry identical reserve percentages, identical owner-occupancy ratios, and identical loss histories. One has deferred $400,000 in waterproofing work for three consecutive budget cycles. The other has not. The lender cannot see the difference. Neither can the borrower. The underwriting treats them as equivalent risks because the documents they produce are equivalent — and documents produced by the institution being evaluated will always reflect what that institution chose to report.

Financial statements tell a story. Reserve studies tell a story. Budgets tell a story. But they do not always tell the full story. What they cannot capture is how the system is performing in real time. Are maintenance issues being addressed consistently, or only when they become urgent? Are communications clear and timely, or do they arrive after decisions have already been made? Are problems surfacing early, or building quietly beneath the surface? These are observable conditions inside every community, and for years they have existed without a structure to make them visible or useful.

This is where a neutral, independent layer of information becomes necessary — one that does not operate the community, does not approve budgets or manage vendors, but aggregates experience from verified participants, presents it in a structured form, and separates information from control. That separation is what gives it credibility. It cannot be produced by the institution being evaluated. It can only be produced by the people living inside it.

THE CTI™ AS AN UNDERWRITING SIGNAL

The CTI™ is not a survey in the traditional sense. It is a structured aggregation of verified homeowner experience across five core dimensions — governance, financial stewardship, maintenance, communication, and emotional trust — collected on a recurring cycle and organized into a signal that persists and compounds over time. A single review reflects an individual experience. A pattern across verified participants, sustained across multiple cycles, reflects a condition within the system. The distinction matters in underwriting because lenders do not make decisions on isolated data points. They look for consistency, repeatability, and correlation.

In the same way that credit scoring transformed borrower evaluation by standardizing individual financial behavior into a comparable metric, the CTI™ introduces a structured framework for evaluating community performance — independent of any single operator, updated on a defined schedule, and increasingly necessary as insurance pressures, regulatory changes, and aging infrastructure widen the gap between communities that appear similar on paper but operate very differently in practice.

For lenders, this layer fills a gap that traditional documents cannot cover. It provides a view into how decisions are being executed and how conditions are evolving between reporting periods. It does not replace financial data. It complements it — answering not just whether a community meets minimum standards, but how it is actually performing over time.

Participation is what converts homeowner experience into a usable signal. When participation is strong, patterns become clearer and the signal becomes more representative. When participation is limited, absence becomes its own condition — not automatically indicating higher risk, but removing the layer of visibility that would otherwise reduce uncertainty. In lending, uncertainty is not neutral. It is priced.

Suppressing participation does not remove risk. It delays visibility. Problems not surfaced early tend to appear later in concentrated form — deferred maintenance becomes large capital projects, communication gaps become conflicts, and unexamined financial assumptions become special assessments that arrive without warning and alter what a borrower can comfortably carry.

COMMUNITY CREDIBILITY AS A LENDING DIMENSION

Lending models rarely change all at once. They evolve as new information becomes available, is tested in practice, and proves useful in reducing uncertainty. The CTI™ enters the lending conversation at this early stage. It does not replace borrower underwriting or override established project approval criteria. It adds a dimension that was previously unavailable: community credibility.

Two borrowers with similar financial profiles may carry different levels of risk depending on the communities they are part of. One may be supported by a well-functioning association with clear communication, proactive maintenance, and stable governance. The other may operate within a system that is less consistent, less transparent, and more reactive. These differences influence probability. And probability is what lending decisions are built on.

In its earliest use, the CTI™ will appear in conversations. A lender reviewing a file may note that a community shows consistent performance across governance, maintenance, and communication. Another may find that participation is limited or that conditions suggest delays in execution — and the underwriting conversation shifts, not because the borrower has changed, but because the environment around the borrower has come into view. As the framework proves consistent, its role expands. It informs questions asked during underwriting. It influences conditions placed on a loan. This is how informal inputs become formal considerations — first informing judgment, then informing process, eventually informing pricing.

Lenders have always priced borrower risk. What comes next is pricing the system around the borrower.

THE SYSTEMIC DIMENSION

There is a broader layer to this discussion that extends beyond individual loans and into the financial system itself. Homeowners associations operate at a scale that is rarely framed correctly. Roughly 375,000 communities govern an estimated $11 trillion in residential property value and administer approximately $140 billion in annual fees. Those fees are not discretionary. They fund the infrastructure that sustains these communities — roofs, roads, elevators, insurance, and the systems that determine whether properties maintain their value over time. From a banking perspective, this is not background. It is exposure.

These associations maintain operating accounts and reserve balances that sit inside the financial system. An HOA reserve account is not a savings account in the traditional sense. It is a forward-looking structure tied to future work that will need to be completed. The question is not whether reserves will be used. It is when. In a well-functioning community, that timing is managed. In a stressed community, timing shifts. Maintenance is deferred. Costs build quietly until they can no longer be delayed. Reserves often appear stable until they are required, and when they move, they move quickly. The balances may look similar on paper. The behavior is not.

Banks do not just hold HOA reserves. They hold the timing risk of how those reserves will be used.

The connection between governance and financial behavior is not always visible in formal documents. These conditions determine whether costs are distributed over time or concentrated into single events. Banks holding HOA reserves should evaluate not just balances but the conditions driving those balances. Governance, maintenance, and participation variability can translate directly into cash flow instability across portfolios. At the institutional level, that difference is material.

This is where the CTI™ connects directly to reserve behavior. The five pillars — governance, financial stewardship, maintenance, communication, and emotional trust — are indicators of how and when capital will be deployed. Strong maintenance practices reduce deferred costs. Clear governance improves decision timing. Effective communication surfaces issues earlier. When these conditions are present, reserves tend to move predictably. When they are not, reserves tend to move suddenly. The CTI™ does not measure balances. It measures the conditions that determine how those balances behave.

At the level of a single community, these dynamics are contained. At the level of 375,000 communities, they are not. If multiple communities show rising costs, deferred maintenance, limited participation, and inconsistent execution simultaneously, the result is not isolated volatility. It is correlated movement. That is where local conditions begin to influence broader financial stability. HOAs are not institutions that fail in a single event. But at $11 trillion in value and $140 billion in annual fees, they are too large to ignore.

Financial reporting shows what has happened. The CTI™ shows what is forming. That distinction closes the gap between condition and consequence.

HOA reserves are not just balances. They are commitments tied to future execution. How those commitments are managed determines how capital moves through the system. At scale, that movement matters. HOA performance is not peripheral to the financial system. It is a system that is only beginning to be measured.

Once better information enters a system, it doesn't get removed. It gets used.

CHAPTER 25

THE POLICY WINDOW

Why 77 million voters, $11 trillion in property value, and a skyrocketing affordability crisis have created the conditions for a federal investment – and the accountability standard that makes it defensible

The bill did not exist yet.

But the conditions that produce legislation were already assembled. A constituency of 77 million. A crisis compounding faster than any state process could address. And — for the first time — a measurement system capable of making accountability auditable at scale.

What was missing was not the problem. The problem had been present for decades, building quietly in the underfunded reserves, the aging infrastructure, the special assessments arriving with increasing frequency, and the property values beginning to reflect what markets eventually price when governance quality becomes visible: that a home inside a poorly governed community is worth less than a home inside a well-governed one.

What was missing was the instrument that makes federal investment in privately governed communities defensible.

That instrument now exists. The data layer the $11 trillion housing market was missing is also the accountability layer the federal policy conversation required.

WHY STATE LEGISLATION WILL NOT SOLVE THIS

The instinct to route HOA reform through state legislatures is understandable. HOA law is state-governed. CC&Rs, board authority, reserve fund requirements, disclosure obligations, assessment powers — all of it lives at the state level. The federal government has no direct regulatory jurisdiction over HOA governance, and fifty years of legal precedent supports that boundary.

But state-by-state reform is not a solution at the scale this problem requires. It is a process — slow, uneven, susceptible to capture by the industry associations whose members fund state legislative campaigns, and structurally incapable of addressing a national affordability crisis on a timeline that matches the urgency.

Florida has been trying to reform its HOA reserve funding requirements for years. The legislation that passed in the wake of the Surfside collapse — the most catastrophic HOA governance failure in American history — was weakened in subsequent sessions by industry lobbying before its compliance deadlines arrived. Texas passed HOA transparency legislation that created new disclosure requirements without creating any mechanism to verify that the disclosures were accurate. California's HOA reform efforts have produced incremental improvements in a state where the scale of the insurance crisis is so acute that incremental improvements are functionally irrelevant.

This is what state-by-state reform produces: decades of effort, partial results, and the systematic erosion of whatever gains survive the next legislative session when the industry associations return with their amendments.

The 77 million Americans living in HOA communities cannot wait for fifty state legislatures to independently arrive at a consistent, enforceable, funded accountability standard. The federal government has the authority to act — not by regulating HOA governance directly, but through the spending power that has shaped every major policy initiative of the last century. Federal money comes with federal conditions. Visibility precedes legitimacy. The conditions that make investment defensible now exist. The path to action runs through them.

THE DOUBLE PAYMENT NOBODY NAMED

There is a financial reality at the center of HOA living that has never been fully named in a policy context, despite being experienced by 77 million Americans every month.

HOA homeowners pay twice.

They pay property taxes that fund the public infrastructure every American relies on — roads, stormwater systems, street lighting, sidewalks, parks, schools, libraries, emergency services. These are the shared systems of civic life, funded collectively and maintained by the governments that collect the taxes.

Then they pay again. The roads inside their community. The stormwater and drainage systems within their development. The street lighting their HOA installed and whose electricity bill their dues pay every month. The sidewalks and internal paths their association maintains. The landscaping of common areas their taxes do not cover. The reserves — every dollar set aside to eventually replace what was built when the development was new, funded entirely by the homeowners inside the community, with no public contribution of any kind.

Seventy-seven million Americans are paying for infrastructure twice — once through taxes and once through dues. That is not a contractual arrangement the federal government can ignore indefinitely. It is a structural inequity at a scale that dwarfs most policy problems Congress has chosen to address.

The federal government has invested in highways, airports, broadband infrastructure, flood protection, and rural electrification — all cases where private benefit and public interest were sufficiently aligned to justify public investment. The case for HOA infrastructure investment is stronger than most of those precedents. The beneficiaries are not corporations or utilities. They are homeowners. Seventy-seven million of them. Paying twice. Asking once.

THE INVESTMENT CASE

The federal investment target of $25 to $30 billion is derived from three specific, addressable components of the HOA affordability and infrastructure crisis — each measurable, each time-limited, each recoverable through the stabilization it produces.

Reserve restoration funding addresses the aggregate shortfall between what HOA reserves currently hold and what they need to hold to fund projected capital replacements without special assessments. Targeted at communities whose reserve funds have fallen below the threshold creating imminent assessment risk — concentrated in Florida, Texas, California, Nevada, and Arizona — this component represents approximately $12 to $15 billion. Its return is direct: eliminated assessment risk produces stabilized property values, restored transaction volume, and a homeowner population no longer absorbing costs the system was never designed to make visible.

Infrastructure rehabilitation addresses the physical condition of HOA community assets whose deferred maintenance has reached a level that threatens property values and resident safety. Parking structures. Waterproofing systems. Roofing. Mechanical systems. Elevators. The shared physical assets that 77 million Americans depend on and that no public infrastructure program has ever addressed. Approximately $8 to $10 billion.

An insurance backstop addresses the market failure compressing HOA affordability in the states where private carrier withdrawal has been most acute — a coverage mechanism of last resort for communities that cannot obtain private coverage at rates compatible with financial health. Approximately $5 to $7 billion.

Together: a $25 to $30 billion system-level correction in $11 trillion of American residential wealth that fifty years of governance without accountability has been quietly eroding. Not a subsidy. A recovery investment in the infrastructure layer the market has been pricing without being able to measure.

VISIBILITY AS INFRASTRUCTURE

Federal investment in HOA infrastructure without an accountability framework is capital deployed into a system that has no mechanism to demonstrate whether it produced the intended outcome. The community that receives federal reserve restoration funding and promptly underfunds the reserve again has absorbed public money without changing the condition that made public money necessary.

The accountability condition is specific: no federal dollar flows to an HOA community without a verified, independent, third-party homeowner performance signal on the public record. Not a self-assessment. Not a management company report. Not a trade association credential. A verified signal — produced by confirmed owners, organized across standardized dimensions, publicly accessible, and updated on a recurring cycle that ensures it reflects current conditions rather than a historical snapshot.

Accountability is a condition, not a policy. What makes it functional here is that the verification does not require a new federal apparatus to administer it. The homeowner is the auditor. The verified signal is the audit. Congress does not need a new agency or a new reporting requirement to verify that communities are deploying federal investment responsibly. The homeowners who live inside the investment are producing the verification in real time, twice a year, on a publicly accessible platform that any constituent, journalist, or oversight committee can consult without a FOIA request.

The drawdown structure ties subsequent tranches to trajectory, not just participation. The community whose verified scores are declining while federal dollars are flowing receives a remediation notification before the next tranche is released. Not a penalty. A feedback loop — the system correcting in the direction the verified signal points.

Federal programs that distribute money without visible accountability metrics are the programs that get cut when the political winds shift. Federal programs that can show, community by community, dimension by dimension, quarter by quarter, where investment produced measurable improvement in verified homeowner experience — those programs build the constituency for continuation. The accountability condition is not just what makes the investment defensible. It is what makes the investment durable.

A NOTE ON COMMUNITIES THAT CANNOT GENERATE PARTICIPATION

The accountability condition raises a legitimate concern: what happens to communities that cannot produce verified participation — newly formed associations without established homeowner relationships, communities with high transience rates, or communities where the governance failures that make federal investment necessary are the same failures that have suppressed homeowner voice for years?

The answer is that the participation threshold must be calibrated to community type, not applied uniformly. A newly turned-over community of eighty units cannot be held to the same participation standard as a ten-year-old community of four hundred. A community in a market with documented suppression history — where homeowners have been discouraged from engaging through the patterns this book has described — requires a pathway that acknowledges the condition rather than penalizing it. The policy framework that excludes the most dysfunctional communities from the investment they need most has not solved the problem. It has transferred it.

What the accountability condition requires is not a participation threshold that functions as a gate. It is a participation structure that functions as a starting condition — one that begins at enrollment and grows toward the standard as investment and governance improvement proceed in parallel. Communities that cannot yet generate verified participation are precisely the communities the investment is designed to reach. The framework serves them by creating the condition — anonymity, protection, independence from the institution being evaluated — that makes honest participation possible for the first time.

THE SECONDARY MARKET LEVER

The most powerful federal action available requires no appropriation. It requires a directive.

Fannie Mae and Freddie Mac are federally controlled entities. A directive from the FHFA requiring verified third-party homeowner performance signal participation as a condition of condo project approval — the warrantability standard that determines whether conventional lenders can originate loans on units in a given community — reshapes the entire HOA market without spending a dollar.

The community that does not participate loses access to conventional financing for its units. The sellers whose buyers cannot finance conventionally face a materially smaller buyer pool and a materially lower market price. The board that receives that market signal has a governance reform incentive more powerful than any bylaw, statute, or certification program has ever produced — because it is priced into the asset the board was elected to protect.

The FHFA already conditions condo project approval on reserve funding adequacy, insurance coverage thresholds, delinquency rate limits, and litigation status. Adding verified homeowner signal participation to that list is an extension of existing authority. The legal pathway is clear. The market impact is direct.

The FHFA directive and the investment bill are not alternative mechanisms. They are sequential ones. The directive creates the participation incentive at the warrantability level. The bill provides the capital communities need to address the conditions the directive and the market are now requiring them to demonstrate. Together they produce an environment in which verified homeowner accountability is not a choice but a structural condition — of federal funding, of conventional financing, and of the property values both protect.

THE WINDOW

Policy windows open when scale, data, and consequence align.

Scale: 77 million homeowners in every competitive congressional district in the country, paying twice, asking once. Data: a verified, standardized, publicly accessible signal of community governance quality that did not exist eighteen months ago. Consequence: a compounding affordability and infrastructure crisis that is suppressing property values, pricing homeowners out of communities they have lived in for decades, and compressing the residential transaction volume the broader economy depends on.

All three are present. The system now produces conditions federal frameworks historically respond to.

The 77 million Americans who have been paying for their own infrastructure while funding everyone else's are waiting to find out whether Washington can see what they have been living with all along.

They have been living with it for fifty years.

The data that makes the bill possible to write well arrived first. The accountability infrastructure that makes the investment defensible exists. The window does not stay open indefinitely.

The bill is waiting to be written.

What the bill requires to be written well is not more evidence of the problem. That evidence has been accumulating for fifty years. What it requires is the standard that makes the investment auditable — and the recognition that the standard does not require the government to build anything. It requires 77 million homeowners, five minutes twice a year, describing what they already know.

CHAPTER 26

THE TIPPING POINT

When the standard becomes the expectation – and what the market looks like on the other side

The listing had been on the market for eleven days.

The unit was right. The neighborhood was right. The price was competitive. By every measure that had defined the home search for the prior fifty years of the HOA era, it should have been generating offers.

It wasn't.

The buyers who had looked at it had asked the same question, in different ways, through different agents. Some had asked their agents directly. Some had searched for the answer before scheduling a showing. Some had arrived at the property already knowing.

Why doesn't this community have a CTI™ score?

It was not an accusatory question. It was not a demand. It was the question that buyers in this market had learned to ask because every comparable community in the same zip code had a verified homeowner record that answered it — and the absence of one had stopped being neutral.

The listing agent called the board chair. The board chair said the community had chosen not to participate. The listing agent was quiet for a moment.

Then she said: that choice is affecting your listings.

The board chair called an emergency meeting.

That is the tipping point. Not a regulation. Not a mandate. Not a federal requirement or a state disclosure law. A listing agent calling a board chair to explain that the market had moved and the community had not.

Once that call happens enough times, in enough markets, the standard is no longer optional. It is the expectation. And the community that declines to meet the expectation is making a statement the market reads with increasing clarity.

The statement is: we would rather not be seen. In a market that can see, that statement has a cost.

HOW STANDARDS BECOME EXPECTATIONS

Every market standard that eventually became unavoidable followed the same arc. It began as an option. Some participants adopted it early. Others watched. The early adopters gained an advantage that was visible to the watchers. The watchers began to adopt. The adoption accelerated. At some point the critical mass shifted — the standard moved from something some participants had to something most participants had — and the community without it stopped being unremarkable and started being conspicuous.

School district ratings. Inspection reports. Walkability scores. Each was, at some point, a new piece of information that some buyers consulted and others ignored. Each is now a standard filter in the home search — so basic to the evaluation of a purchase that its absence would be considered a gap in the process. Nobody removed them when some neighborhoods scored poorly. They became the mechanism by which neighborhoods that scored poorly were held accountable to the buyers who could now see the score.

In 2026, the community without a score is unremarkable in most markets. In 2028, the absence means something in markets where participation has reached critical mass. In 2031, the absence is a red flag in every major HOA market in the country. The community that has chosen invisibility in a market where visibility is the norm is communicating something the market has learned to read accurately: that what visibility would reveal is something the community would rather the market not see.

The arc does not reverse. Standards do not un-become standards. Invisibility was never neutral. It just had no cost until the market could see who was choosing it.

THE BOARD THAT WAITED TOO LONG

There is a specific failure mode in the adoption arc of every market standard — the participant who watches others adopt, concludes the standard applies to everyone but them, and discovers the cost of that conclusion at the moment the market makes it unavoidable.

In the governance visibility arc, that board is the one that chose invisibility while comparable communities were building verified records. It dismissed the signal as unproven while buyers in its market were incorporating it into their search filters. It said we have always governed this community well and one report is not going to change that — and then received the listing agent's call eleven days into a listing that should have generated offers.

The board that waited too long is not necessarily a board that governed poorly. Some of these boards governed well. Some maintained their infrastructure, funded their reserves, and treated their homeowners with the transparency and fairness that the governance dimensions measure. The problem they face is not that the score would be bad. It is that they have no score.

In a market where the verified record is the expectation, the absence of a record is not neutrality. It is an unanswered question. And unanswered questions, in transactions that involve the largest financial commitment most buyers will ever make, generate a specific anxiety that produces eleven days on the market without an offer.

The path forward is the same regardless of governance quality: participate, build the record, and let the verified homeowner experience speak for what the board has been doing. For the board that governed well and waited, the path is simply delayed recognition. For the board that governed poorly and waited, the path requires governance improvement before the record it builds reflects what the market needs to see.

The alternative — continued invisibility in a market where visibility is the norm — is not a strategy. It is an accelerating liability.

THE $28 BILLION THAT PARTICIPATION RECOVERS

Forty million HOA-encumbered homes in the United States. One hundred forty billion dollars in annual dues. At the higher end of informed estimates, the annual cost of governance without accountability approaches $28 billion — derived from applying standard inefficiency ranges for unaccountable managed-service systems to the $140 billion the HOA market administers annually. The figure represents the accumulated cost of procurement opacity, deferred maintenance conversion, reserve misalignment, and avoidable legal and operational expenses. The figure is an estimate. The mechanism producing it is not.

The system was not designed to waste money. It was designed to manage shared infrastructure at scale. But the way it operates in practice introduces structural inefficiencies. Board turnover interrupts long-term planning before consequences materialize. Management company portfolio models reduce community-specific knowledge. Decisions are made in fragments, without a continuous feedback loop tying outcome to accountability. What appears as waste is not the result of intent. It is the result of structure — the ordinary operation of a system that was never required to measure its own performance.

That inefficiency lives in specific places. Procurement opacity — vendor contracts awarded through management company networks rather than competitive processes, communities paying above-market prices for adequate work because the competition that would have benchmarked those prices was removed before the board ever saw the proposals. Uninformed board decision-making — volunteer boards making capital decisions using processes designed to appear competitive without producing competition. And deferred maintenance compounding — the $30,000 repair that becomes $80,000 because successive boards deferred it in the name of dues stability.

Each of these looked reasonable at the time it was made. Together they represent the accumulated cost of governance without consequence. Visible costs have consequences. Consequences change behavior. Changed behavior, across 40 million homes, begins to recover the estimate that the absence of accountability has been costing homeowners annually.

The recovery is not dramatic. It is incremental. One procurement decision. One maintenance decision. One board acting on a signal earlier than it would have without it. Each of these is a small number. Aggregated across 40 million homes, they are not.

WHAT THE MARKET LOOKS LIKE ON THE OTHER SIDE

Buyers filter by governance score before they schedule showings. Lenders incorporate the signal into day-one underwriting. Management companies compete on demonstrated performance. Boards govern with external accountability. The RFP process has a benchmark.

The infrastructure decisions that have been accumulating waste for decades are being made with information they were never made with before. The board considering a major capital project can see what comparable communities paid and how those outcomes were experienced. The vendor that priced to win rather than to perform has a record the board can consult before the contract is signed.

That is the market on the other side of the tipping point. Not a different system. The same system, finally able to see what it has always been doing — and facing, for the first time, the consequences of what it sees.

THE SYSTEM THAT CORRECTS ITSELF

The most important feature of a self-reinforcing standard is not what it does to participants performing poorly. It is what it does to participants performing well.

The community that has been governing with integrity has been doing so without the market being able to see it. On the other side of the tipping point, the distinction is visible. The well-governed community has a verified score that tells every buyer, every lender, and every realtor exactly what its homeowners have been experiencing. The property values in that community reflect the governance quality that produced them.

The light the early chapters of this book described is on now. It was built by homeowners who decided their experience was worth recording. It does not turn off.

The tipping point is not coming. For the communities paying attention, it is already here.

The question it leaves open is not whether the standard arrives. It is whether your community is part of it when it does.

CHAPTER 27

THE HOMEOWNER DECISION

The system will not fix itself. But it will follow the people who decide to fix it.

The community that governs well has always existed. What it has never had is proof.

The CTI™ is the proof.

You have read the full argument now.

You know what the system is, how it was designed, and how it drifted. You understand what $11 trillion in residential wealth looks like when it is governed without a performance standard — underfunded reserves, deferred maintenance, special assessments that arrive without warning, boards that govern without consequence, and buyers who close without knowing what they are buying into.

You know what the CTI™ is, how it works, and why a verified homeowner review carries a weight no institutional report can replicate.

You understand the system. Understanding is not the same as changing it. Changing it requires one more condition.

YOUR IDENTITY IS NEVER REVEALED

Before anything else, this needs to be clear.

When you submit a CTI™ review, your name does not appear anywhere — not on the score, not in the comments, and not in any report that reaches the board, the management company, the buyer, the lender, or any external party. Your identity is protected. What is verified is that you own a unit in the community you are reviewing — not who you are, but that you live there and that your experience is real.

The structure is simple. Ownership is confirmed. Identity is protected. Experience becomes part of the record. That protection is not incidental. It is what makes honest participation possible in a system where speaking up has historically carried risk.

THE ONE THING THAT MAKES IT REAL

Every argument in this book rests on a single condition: that the verified homeowner experience exists at scale. Not the concept. Not the platform. The actual, submitted account of what it is like to live in your community.

That account does not exist until it is written.

The score a buyer reads is the aggregation of homeowners who chose to participate. The benchmark a board compares itself against is built from those same inputs. The management company record is not what it reports about itself — it is what homeowners describe across the communities it serves.

Every signal comes from the same place: a homeowner who took the time to describe what they experienced.

WHAT ELEVEN MINUTES PRODUCES

The review takes eleven minutes, twice a year. In that time, you answer structured questions about governance, financial stewardship, maintenance, communication, and trust. You describe what you have seen, and you submit.

Your input joins others. The pattern becomes visible. The signal forms. Eleven minutes, twice a year, is the participation cost of the most consequential accountability standard the HOA market has ever had.

WHAT YOUR SILENCE COSTS

You have already experienced this system. The request that went unanswered. The meeting where the outcome was already decided. The number that arrived without context.

None of these moments felt decisive on their own. Each one was small. Each one was explainable. Together, they changed behavior.

Over time, the expectation that the system would respond disappeared. Not because people stopped caring, but because the system taught them that caring did not change the outcome. From the outside, that looks like apathy. From the inside, it is something else — ownership without influence.

The homeowner who submits a review does not change that history. They change what the next homeowner inherits.

WHAT HAPPENS WHEN YOU LOOK

When you participate, your community's verified record becomes visible to you — the scores across each dimension, the board and management company results evaluated separately, and the trajectory over time. For most homeowners, the result is immediate. They either recognize what they have been experiencing or they see something they had not fully understood before. In both cases, the effect is the same. The system becomes visible. And a system that is visible can be improved.

THE NEXT PERSON

There is someone who will come after you. They will evaluate your community without knowing what you have experienced unless that experience is made visible. You are the only person who can provide that clarity.

What you submit becomes permanent. It is the record the next buyer reads before making an offer. It is the signal the board cannot dismiss when it arrives from twenty verified homeowners rather than one frustrated voice in a meeting. It is the data point that, aggregated across communities and quarters, begins to move the market in the direction accountability always moves it: toward the governance quality the signal rewards.

THE DECISION

The system now exists. The signal is forming. The market is learning to read it. The remaining question is whether your community becomes part of that signal.

Participation does not require agreement with every governance decision your board has made. It requires an honest account of what you have experienced. A system that can be seen can be improved. A system that cannot be seen continues as it is.

The system will not fix itself. It will follow the people who make it visible.

WHAT HAPPENS NEXT

Well-governed communities have always existed. What they lacked was proof. That condition has changed.

The signal now exists. The market can see it. Once it can see it, it begins to respond — not through policy, but through behavior. The communities that can be seen are trusted. The communities that cannot be seen are questioned. The difference between the two compounds over time.

The light is on now, and it does not turn off.

The CTI™ is the proof. The market will do the rest.

The system was never designed to waste the accumulated cost of fifty years of governance without consequence. It was designed without the feedback mechanism that would have made that cost visible — and invisible cost, in any system at any scale, accumulates until someone builds the instrument to measure it. That instrument now exists. The rest is eleven minutes.

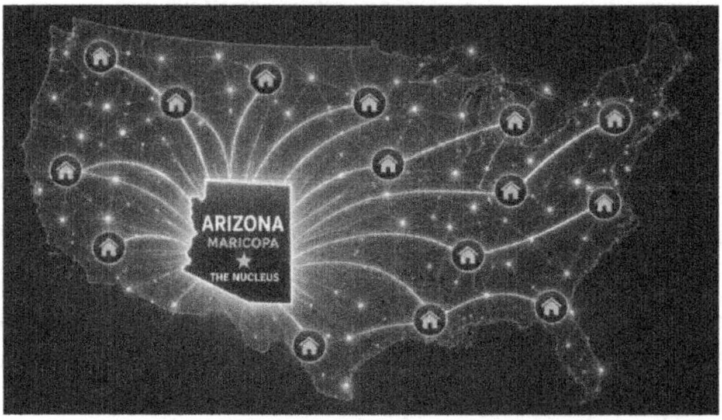

Arizona. Maricopa. The Nucleus. It starts here.

Your community's score doesn't exist yet.

Every HOA in America starts at zero. The only way a score gets built

is when homeowners who live there submit a verified review.

Yours takes eleven minutes.

HOADoctor.com

Start your review.

No names shown. We verify your ownership.

The first 1,000 homeowners earn permanent Founders Circle status.

Arizona first. Then everywhere.

ABOUT THE AUTHOR

Bill McKay created the first standardized trust signal for HOA governance—bringing visibility to one of the largest blind spots in the U.S. housing market.

More than 77 million Americans live in HOA-governed communities, representing over $11 trillion in residential value. Until now, there has been no consistent way to measure how these communities are actually run.

He served for seven years on the Master Association Board of the Arizona Biltmore Estates Village Association (ABEVA), overseeing seventeen sub-associations, and led a $1.87 million community transformation.

He also led a successful board recall as a homeowner, gaining experience on both sides of HOA governance.

McKay is a serial entrepreneur with multiple exits, including transactions involving private equity and Sumitomo Corporation of America.

He created the Community Trust Index™ (CTI™) and founded HOA Doctor™, a platform designed to bring transparency and accountability to HOA communities nationwide.

HOAs Unmasked is both an exposé and a call to action—marking the beginning of a broader shift toward visibility, accountability, and trust.

ACKNOWLEDGMENTS

This book was not written in isolation. It was shaped by conversations, experiences, and perspectives from people across the country—homeowners, board members, property managers, real estate professionals, and others who have lived inside this system in different ways.

To the homeowners who shared their stories—openly, and sometimes quietly—thank you. Your experiences, frustrations, and insights brought clarity to a system that too often operates without it.

To the homeowners and board members who participated in focus groups—your willingness to compare experiences and challenge assumptions helped refine this work.

To the board members who take the role seriously—who prepare, learn, and carry the responsibility of stewardship with integrity—your work often goes unseen.

To the board members who recognize that governance is not authority alone, but responsibility to the people who fund it—you set the standard this system is capable of meeting.

Not all experiences reflect that standard. This work is shaped by both what is working—and what is not.

To the property managers working in the middle—your perspective is essential. The system does not function without you.

Leaders within management companies will shape the future of this industry by embracing transparency, performance, and accountability at scale.

To the real estate professionals, your insight sharpened the urgency behind this work.

The data and platform professionals shaping modern real estate have made nearly every aspect of the property visible. This book builds on that foundation.

To my LinkedIn community, your engagement and feedback helped refine these ideas in real time.

These conversations pointed to a simple truth: nearly every aspect of a home can be measured and understood except how the community itself is governed.

To the HOA Doctor™ team, this would not exist without you.

To my friends and family, thank you for your belief.

To homeowner advocates and legislators, your efforts continue to move this system forward.

To the early supporters of HOA Doctor™—your input mattered more than you know.

And finally, to the readers, this is the point where the conversation begins.

TRADEMARKS & ATTRIBUTION

HOA Doctor™ is a trademark of Doc Vault Inc.

Community Trust Index™ (CTI™) and related marks are trademarks of Doc Vault Inc.

All other trademarks are the property of their respective owners.

DISCLAIMER

This book is intended for informational and educational purposes only and does not constitute legal, financial, real estate, or other professional advice.

The content is based on personal experience, research, and aggregated observations and is not intended as a substitute for advice from qualified professionals. Readers should consult appropriate legal, financial, or real estate professionals regarding their specific circumstances.

While reasonable efforts have been made to ensure accuracy, no representations or warranties are made regarding the completeness, reliability, or applicability of the information to any particular community, jurisdiction, or situation.

No guarantees are made regarding outcomes based on the concepts or frameworks presented in this book. Conditions, regulations, and practices may vary significantly across jurisdictions and may change over time.

The author and publisher disclaim any liability for decisions made or actions taken based on the information provided.

Made in the USA
Coppell, TX
10 June 2026

80119276R00134